M000202402

HAVANA

A pocket guide to the city's best
cultural hangouts, shops, bars
and eateries

**CLAIRE
BOOBBYER**

Hardie Grant

TRAVEL

CONTENT/

INTRODUCTION

Havana will seduce you, I guarantee it. It's the music, the fun-loving locals with their razor-sharp wit, the layered, oddball history, the beautiful mansions and Art Deco towers in gelati colours, the coloured American cars in potholed streets, and a raw, creative energy and can-do ethos in the face of scarcities, political hurdles and hardships.

You might come looking for the city 'frozen in time', the last bastion of communism in the Western hemisphere. You'll see the collapsing urban scenery amid the colonial squares of urban revival in Old Havana (thanks to the work of the City Historian's Office and UNESCO protection), and you might be convinced you've travelled back in time to the '50s. But I urge you to park that narrative when you land, and dig deep beyond the patina of distressing decay and the lackadaisical service you might encounter at a state-run hotel or restaurant.

Fidel Castro's 1959 Revolution spearheaded literacy and free education and today Cuba's population is highly educated, loquacious, lyrical, pedantic even. Sport and culture are highly favoured and legions of Habaneros are virtuosos of music, literature, film, dance and art. At subsidised prices you can catch world-class concerts and art shows. Correction: you can gorge on a smorgasbord of Cuban culture at unthinkable prices back home.

Almost 10 years ago, ex-president Raúl Castro opened the door to greater private enterprise, allowing thousands to open restaurants, cafes and boutique apartments. This act revived Havana. Today, you'll find new cocktail bars, music haunts, shops selling designer wares, artists' studios, art installations, street murals, passionate chefs at paladares (private restaurants) and gorgeous light-filled apartments and casas (homestays). This guide will deliver you to these many public and hidden doors in this extraordinary 500-year-old city.

When you want languorous palm trees, tinkling waterfalls and teal pools, a horse ride through a sun-drenched limestone valley, mountain air, birds and flowers, home-cooked organic lunches, coral reef and periwinkle seas, head out of Havana to the Field Trips, which you'll find at the back of this book.

Havana's magic is infectious. The city will make you want to return.

Claire Boobbyer

A PERFECT HAVANA DAY

My perfect day in Havana begins with coffee, either at **El Café** or **Lo de Monik**, and kickstarting the day with one of their breakfasts – the best egg and toast combos in the Old Town. Catch the latest show at **Museo de Bellas Artes (Arte Cubano)**, then wander – part purposefully, part aimlessly – through the busy colourful streets with pregoneros (singing sellers) calling out their wares, and over the cobblestones to see the latest aristocratic mansions restored to their former glory. Browse new shops **Dador**, **Memorias**, **Capicúa** and **Clandestina** opened by the city's entrepeneurs, and telescope in on street details – pretty patterned tiles, fancy brass doorknobs, neon signs, a shop name embedded in terrazzo paving. Visit **Factoría Habana** for its latest hot-names exhibition. Hop in a pedicab to visit emerging arty **San Isidro Distrito de Arte** in the southern part of the old city, taking in the striking street murals. Stop for a drink at **Bar Jesús María 20** or **Jibaro**. For lunch, pull up a chair at **El Dandy** for pork tacos while people-watching over Plaza del Cristo. After lunch, hail an almendrón (American classic car) and head to **El Vedado** to catch a gallery show, and lose yourself in the faded splendour of the quiet streets wondering who lived in the elegant villas before they became swanky embassies, institutes or schools. After a smoothie at **Belview ArtCafé**, head into the jumbled streets of **Centro Havana** to take photos in the late afternoon golden light, or walk down colonnaded **Prado** to the **Malecón**. Climb to **Nazdarovie** or **Malecón 663** for a sunset cocktail. After dressing up back at your casa (homestay), head to one of Havana's top paladares (private restaurants) for dinner. Go for drinks at **Michifú** or **El del Frente**. Check out what's on and take your picks – whether it's dance at the **Gran Teatro de La Habana Alicia Alonso**, a secret HAPE party at **Estudio 50**, or a gig at **La Casa de la Bombilla Verde** or **Fábrica de Arte Cubano**. Salsa dancers should keep one eye on the billing at **Salsa 1830**. Be flexible with the Cuban night and don't try to cram it all in. There's always tomorrow to embrace the 365-day rich cultural calendar of the city.

POCKET TOP PICKS

TOP ATTRACTIONS

TOP SHOPS

BEST CHEAP EATS

TOP LIVE MUSIC VENUES

BEST BARS

INSPIRING ARCHITECTURE

TOP RESTAURANTS

BEST CITY VIEWS

TOP ARTY SPOTS

HAVANA OVERVIEW

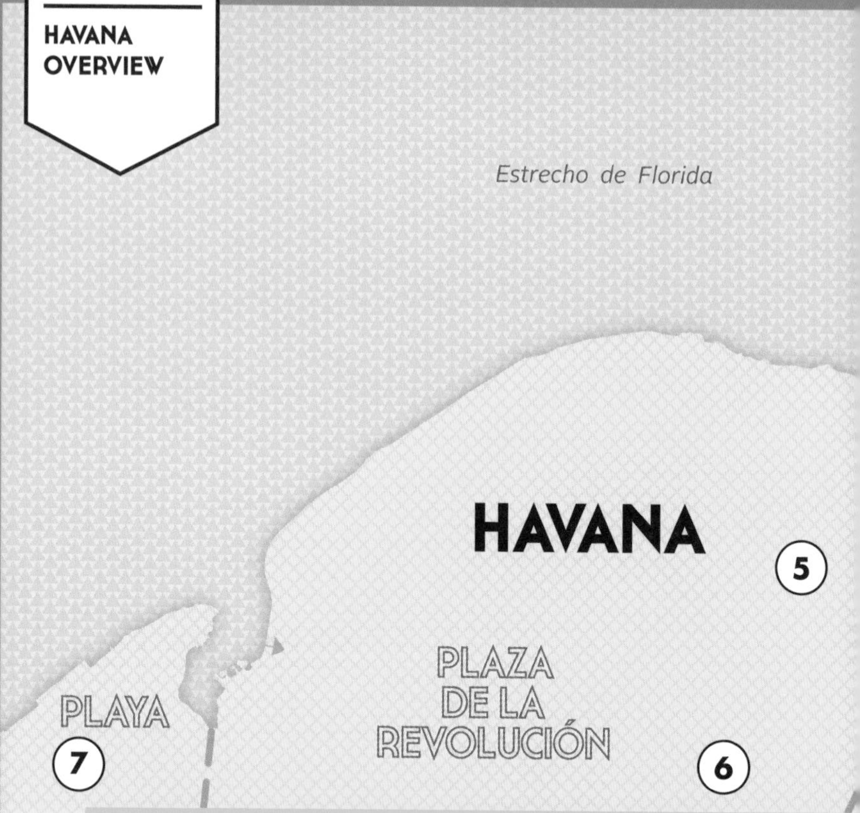

Estrecho de Florida
HAVANA
5
PLAZA DE LA REVOLUCIÓN
6
PLAYA
7

PRECINCTS

FIELD TRIPS

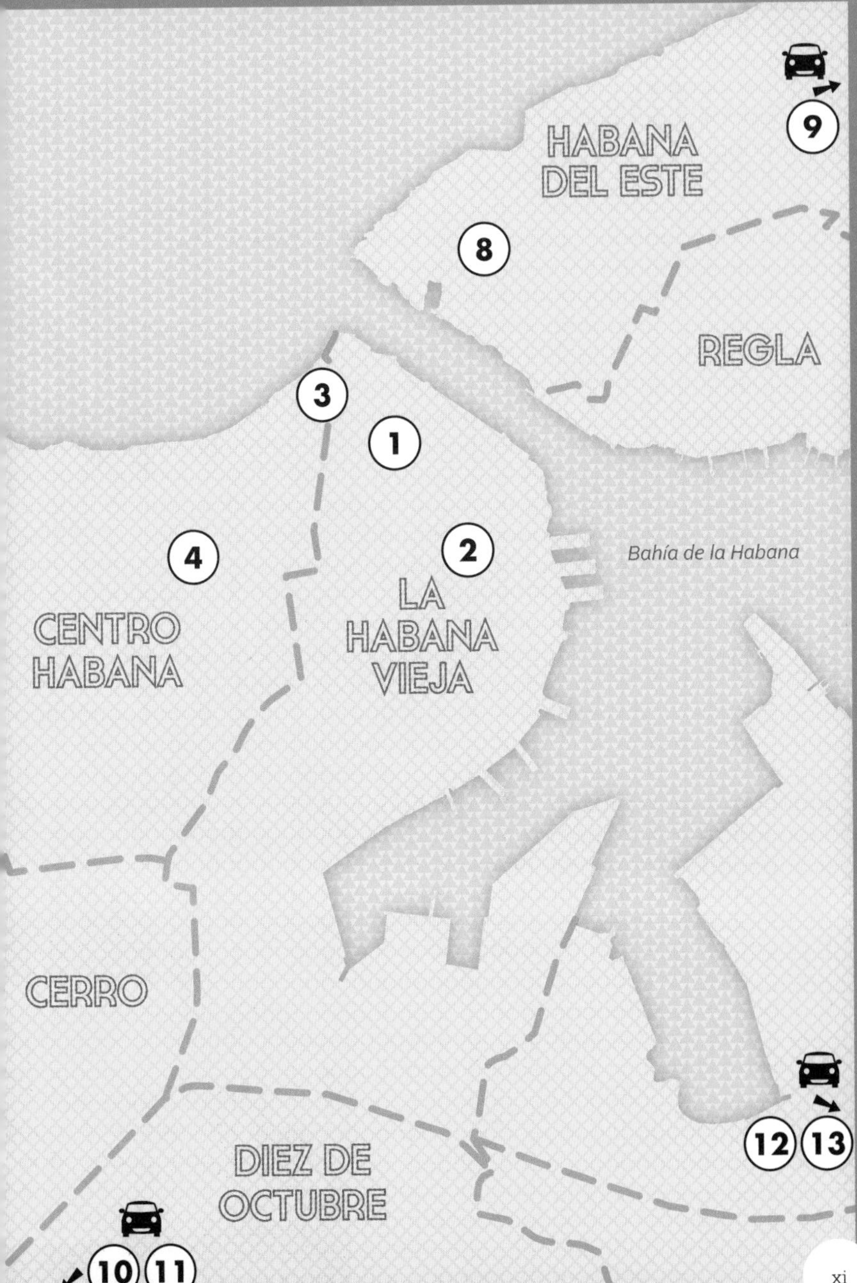

HABANA DEL ESTE

REGLA

Bahía de la Habana

CENTRO HABANA

LA HABANA VIEJA

CERRO

DIEZ DE OCTUBRE

1
2
3
4
8
9
10
11
12
13

NORTHERN OLD HAVANA

With all its tattered beauty, Old Havana is the most intriguing part of the city. Its magnificent buildings were built for the glory of empire and the glory of God. Across several centuries, Cuba's Spanish colonial elite erected Baroque churches, pretty patios, tinkling fountains, handsome civic mansions and fine villas, all linked by huge shadeless squares and tight narrow streets. Plundered silver from Spain's South American colonies passed through Havana. Chests were roped down on the so-called Treasure Fleets, which then crossed the Atlantic to Seville and city rulers built fortresses to protect the loot from pirates. Three castles protect Havana; a fourth, La Cabaña, was erected after the British captured Havana in 1762.

After Fidel Castro's 1959 revolution, Old Havana slumped into a ruinous state. But its 1982 UNESCO protection has brought a patchwork restoration program to Havana's historic core: plazas repaired and mansions revived and turned into museums, hotels and restaurants. But it wasn't until a few years ago when private business was given greater freedoms in Cuba, and the semi-autonomous City Historian's office began to let out premises, that Old Havana emerged from austerity to become a vibrant centre, with restaurants, cafes, bars, boutique B&Bs and shops.

It's a gorgeous place to stay and by day is lively, musical, noisy, intensely interesting and a photographer's dream. By midnight it is dead, with the exception of a few bars. Large swathes are inaccessible to motor traffic so Old Havana is best explored on foot. For this book, Old Havana has been divided into north of pedestrian boulevard Calle Obispo, and south of it (see p. 22).

⇥ A book at the Books and Curios Market, featuring Julio A Mella, co-founder of Cuba's Communist Party

BLAS ROCA

A Mella

1

1 PLAZA DE ARMAƒ & AROUND

Begin your walk at Havana's oldest square, the 1582-founded **Plaza de Armas**, where each November, locals circle a ceiba tree to make a wish in the garden of **El Templete**. This memorial hall commemorates the founding of the city, and first Mass on 16 November 1519. The leafy Plaza de Armas is surrounded by **Castillo de la Real Fuerza** (*see* p. 9); neighbouring **Palacio del Segundo Cabo** (Palace of the Lieutenant–Governor), now a high-tech museum on Cuban–European relations; the Cuban Baroque **Palacio de los Capitanes Generales**; and the handsome **Hotel Santa Isabel**. Gigantes (entertainers on stilts) regularly wander up and down Havana's old city streets around here. West, along Calle Obispo, you'll see the incongruous glass structure of **Colegio de San Gerónimo**, which fills the whole of the site of the city's original 1728 university location. On the left, you'll see **Farmacia Taquechel**, a working pharmacy and a museum capsule of an 1898 dispensary, with dark wood shelves housing dozens of ceramic jars of medicine.

2 PLAZA DE LA CATEDRAL

Calle Empedrado e/San
Ignacio y Mercaderes
7861 7771
Mon–Fri 9.30am–4.30pm,
Sat–Sun 9am–12pm. Sun Mass,
tower closed
[MAP p. 172 C2]

With bougainvillea, half-moon stained-glass windows, cobblestones and coral-encrusted buildings, Old Havana's cathedral square is a sensational homage to Spain's colonial power. The **Catedral de San Cristóbal**, which dominates, was described by writer Alejo Carpentier in the 19th century as 'music set in stone'. It was built by the Jesuits in 1727 but completed by the Franciscans. Look closely to see marine fossils embedded in the Cuban Baroque exterior. Generally open in the mornings, it's most atmospheric when there is evening Mass as the interior lighting illuminates the gull-grey square. The former **Royal Treasury** (Palacio del Marqués de Arcos), military governor's mansion (Palacio de los Condes de Casa Bayona), now the **Museo de Arte Colonial**, and Casa de los Marqueses de Aguas Claras dominate. The Cathedral **bell tower** costs CUC$1 to climb.

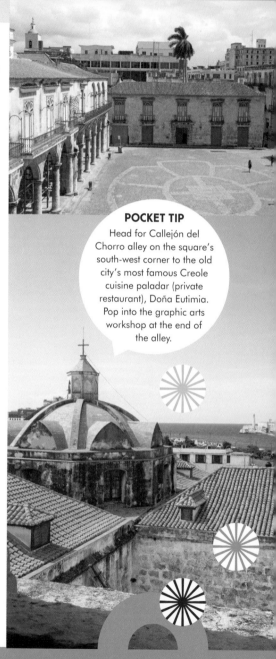

POCKET TIP

Head for Callejón del Chorro alley on the square's south-west corner to the old city's most famous Creole cuisine paladar (private restaurant), Doña Eutimia. Pop into the graphic arts workshop at the end of the alley.

3 MU∫EO DE LA CIUDAD (MU∫EUM OF THE CITY)

Calle Tacón 1 e/Calle Obispo y O'Reilly
7869 7358
Tues–Sun 9.30am–4pm
[MAP p. 173 E3]

Spanish colonial power was centred in this enormous Cuban Baroque mansion furnished and decorated with what huge sums of gold could buy. As the seat of the governor-generals of Cuba from 1791 until 1898, and then the Republic until 1920, its lavish rooms display chandeliers, Carrara marble baths, Sèvres porcelain, and busts of moose, antelope and boar. Its name is a misnomer though; it's more of a collection of historic items and furniture than museum of the city. Come late morning or early afternoon to avoid the crowds. I recommend the new audio guides and you should photograph the museum layout posted on the wall to the left of the entrance to aid your audio guide visit; not every room number is advertised. The museum faces Plaza de Armas (*see* p. 2). Entry is CUC$3, or CUC$5 with an audio guide or guide.

5

4 EDIFICIO BACARDÍ

Calle San Juan de Dios,
esq Calle Monserrate.
Lobby Mon–Sun 8am–6pm
Cafe Mon–Sun 8am–4pm
[MAP p. 181 B1]

The 1930s Art Deco headquarters of the Bacardí rum company is a stunner. It's one of the best-dressed buildings in the city and it knows it. Some 12-storeys high, and crowned by a ziggurat and a bronze bat motif – the famous rum's iconic logo – it towers and shimmers over the edge of Old Havana. The exterior is clad in red and pink granite from Bavaria, and dark granite from Norway. Metal work is embedded with the letter 'B', and bat logos embellish door panels. A decorated frieze of enamelled terracotta panels, featuring naked nymphs by American artist Maxfield Parrish, bands the upper floors. The original mezzanine **cafe** – with painted doors and Art Deco lamps – has been restored. There's no Bacardí rum on the menu but the Havana Club tragos (drinks) are reasonably priced; the coffee is sensibly priced, too. It's also one of the few quiet spots in the city for a drink.

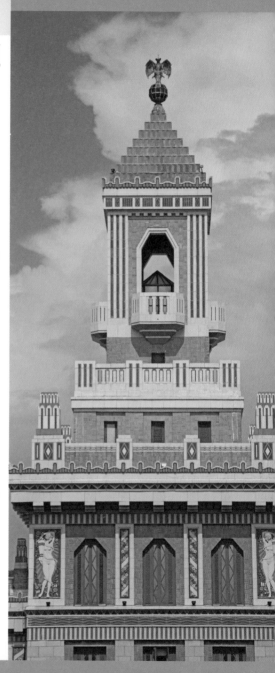

POCKET TIP
Take the elevator to the fifth-floor terrace of nearby Hotel Plaza for the best viewpoint for a fabulous photograph of the upper floors of the Bacardí building.

5 RAÚL CORRALEꟼ GALERÍA

O'Reilly 524 e/Monserrate y Villegas
7801 4617
Tues–Sat 10am–6pm
[MAP p. 181 B1]

A small posse of photographers, christened the Epic Revolution Photographers, were responsible for one of the greatest PR coups of the 20th century – the making of Fidel Castro and his 1959 rebel-fought revolution. I interviewed one of them a few years ago and he complained there was no museum to their endeavour. Now there's a beginning here at the gallery set up by photographer Raúl Corrales' granddaughter, Claudia Corrales, a photographer in her own right. Raúl Corrales was Castro's official photographer from 1959 to 1961. Corrales also captured Che Guevara and Ernest Hemingway in black and white shots. Many of these can be viewed in the gallery. An additional salon showcases rotating exhibits of contemporary Cuban photographers, a welcome addition to the photography scene in Cuba. Check talks and events on its Facebook page.

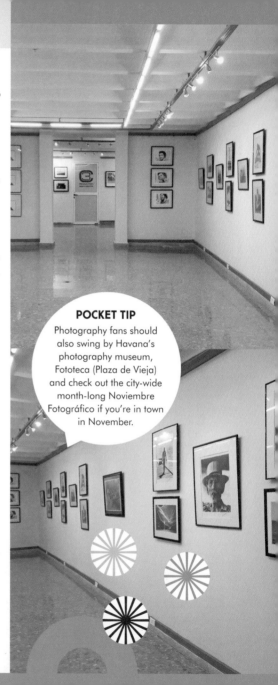

POCKET TIP
Photography fans should also swing by Havana's photography museum, Fototeca (Plaza de Vieja) and check out the city-wide month-long Noviembre Fotográfico if you're in town in November.

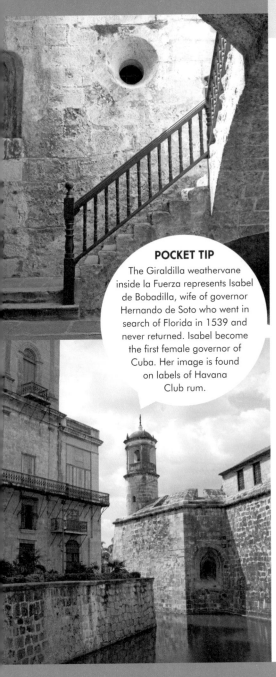

6 CASTILLO DE LA REAL FUERZA

Plaza de Armas
Tues–Sun 9.30am–5pm
[MAP p. 173 E2]

POCKET TIP

The Giraldilla weathervane inside la Fuerza represents Isabel de Bobadilla, wife of governor Hernando de Soto who went in search of Florida in 1539 and never returned. Isabel become the first female governor of Cuba. Her image is found on labels of Havana Club rum.

This pint-sized castle's a classic – chunky walls, a drawbridge, a moat and the lingering ghosts of daredevil buccaneers. Built after French pirate Jacques de Sores (aka 'The Exterminating Angel') burnt the city's first Old Fort in 1555, it was home to the Spanish governors for centuries. Today it houses an under-promoted shipwreck museum. More than 2000 Spanish galleons lie on the seabed around the island – casualties of the *real* pirates of the Caribbean, foul weather and coral reef. It's a shame the display texts are not in English (and there are no guides), but you'll love the exquisite models of Spanish galleons (the *Santísima Trinidad* being the standout), the treasure chests and the dazzling finds from the deep: a carved 16th-century crossbow of iron, wood and vegetable fibre, wine bottles, gold and ruby rings and opal buttons. Upstairs there's a new bilingual film on the 500-year history of boat making at the Royal Arsenal – now the site of the main railway station – and there are sweeping views of Havana's harbour. Castle entry is CUC$3.

7 ARTECORTE, BARBER'S SALON, MUSEUM & ALLEY

Callejón de los Peluqueros
Calle Aguiar e/Tacón y
Peña Pobre
[MAP p. 171 E2]

Turn into Calle Aguiar, and you might think you've stumbled into Barcelona with tables and parasols and plenty of punters enjoying beers. I credit grassroots organisation Artecorte for not only reviving this alley but revitalising a network of streets in this part of the Old Town. Check out the gorgeous neon Artecorte sign while you're here. Community project Artecorte offers hairdressing, bartending and manicure training to unemployed young adults. Havana Club rum sponsors the bartending program and the National Bartending Association helps finds jobs for graduates. Gilberto Valladares (aka 'Papito') founded Artecorte and runs his barber's salon – under the same name – surrounded by vintage hairdressing tools. Antique brushes, retro hair dryers and preserved chairs are displayed around the tiled salon. You can tour the salon with project manager Camilo Condis (see: artecorte.org/en/airbnb). You can also dine at **Restaurant El Figaro**, which contributes the most to Artecorte's project.

POCKET TIP

Fancy an ice-cream? Head to nearby Cuban–French-run Helad'oro (Aguiar 206) for mojito ice-cream; my favourite is the tropical fruit mamey flavor.

8 FACTORÍA HABANA

Calle O'Reilly 308 e/Habana y Aguiar
7864 9518
[MAP p. 172 A4]

This beautifully restored paper factory often holds exciting, crowd-pulling exhibitions and is well worth visiting. The space is set over three floors and supported by wrought-iron classical pillars. Curator Concha Fontenla's last show for the 2019 Habana Bienal – *Intersecciones* – featured work by some of Cuba's greatest: brothers Iván and Yoan Capote, Tonel, José Toirac and Carlos Garaicoa. Travellers don't need to book ahead and all exhibits are free.

9 PI*COLABI*

Calle San Ignacio 75 e/Callejón
del Chorro y O'Reilly
5843 3219
Mon–Sun 9.30am–7.30pm
[MAP p. 172 C3]

Cuba's emerging artisans showcase and sell their work at this attractive self-styled bazaar. The upcycled gifts and crafts here are for travellers looking for something different to Havana's regular souvenirs. Fashion design graduate Sandra de Huelbes and architect Maria Benito realised a dream; and their store, right on a main Old Havana street, has been extremely successful. They source products made from recycled materials found by Cuban creatives all over the city. Look out for lamp bases made from old beer bottles, jewellery and clothing. There's also small metal-crafted work made by famous artist JEFF and the work of painter and designer Eira Arrate y Estela Estevez of Reforma Estudio, whose painted horse figurines are made from old wooden doors and fences. My favourite are the greeting cards and prints of the illustrator Agnes Fong who inks scenes of the city and colourful renditions of fish and fruit.

POCKET TIP
In this part of the old city, skip expensive drinks at Hotel Santa Isabel, lacklustre service at the rooftop bar of nearby Ambos Mundos Hotel, and head around the corner to coffee-scented Café O'Reilly for a reviving Cuban cup of caffeine.

10 FERIA DE PUBLICACIONE/ Y CURIO/IDADE/ (BOOK/ & CURIO/ MARKET)

Calle Baratillo e/Obispo y Justíz
Mon–Sun 8.30am–6pm
[MAP p. 173 F3]

Memorabilia fans should swing by this small market where you can pick up vintage watches, cameras, pins, swizzle sticks, stamps, sepia photos and all manner of Cuban revolution collectibles. Its main focus is books – mostly in Spanish, but there are English language tomes, too. It's a wonderful place to browse and if you're looking for something specific, just ask. My favourite buys have been Cuban Revolution pins, a book bought for its bold graphic cover of a revolutionary, a paper fan-cum-Batista-electoral-propaganda and a heavy brass engraving slab for cigar branding. Note that sellers work alternate days so it's worth visiting twice for further hunting. These sellers are those that used to work around the Plaza de Armas (*see* p. 2) until they were swept here, around the corner. Bargain with a smile. Also note that it's cash only.

POCKET TIP

One of Havana's most bizarre sights lies close by: the Diana, Princess of Wales memorial garden, paid for by the British Embassy.

13

11 LO DE MONIK

Calle Chacón esq Compostela
7864 4029
Mon–Sun 8am–9.30pm, drinks
until 10.30pm
[MAP p. 171 E4]

Looking for breakfast in
northern Old Havana? Look
no further. The chive-flecked
fried egg and bacon CUC$5
breakfast at Lo de Monik is the
best in this part of the city. Its
French crepes with honey are
pretty darn good, too. Settle
in, people-watch from its great
big windows overlooking a
busy corner of the old city,
and head out well and truly
fuelled for sightseeing. Mónica
del Risco Fernández, an
accountant-turned-candy-
maker, opened this very cool
spot with partner Carlos in
2018. Their seafood – octopus
and ceviche fish – is sourced
from Cuban waters and their
vegetables from Havana's top
organic farm, Finca Marta.
Vegetarians will appreciate
the veg tacos, hummus and
spicy yucas bravas – a riff on
Spain's famous tapas dish
patatas bravas.

POCKET TIP

One block north is the small, atmospheric Plazuela de Santo Ángel dominated by the Iglesia Santo Ángel Custodio, where José Martí was baptised.

TRANSITO

12 IVAN CHEFƒ JUƒTO

Calle Aguacate 9 e/Chacón y Tejadillo
7863 9697
Mon–Sun 12pm–12am
[MAP p. 171 E4]

This restaurant's lechoncito – the succulent tender roast suckling pig with a fabulous ridge of crackling – has brought royalty, Hollywood celebs and visitors fast through its door. I'm a fan of their roast squid and seafood risottos too. The small 1776-built home restaurant with its sea blue Mudéjar ceiling is all frilly lampshades, hanging plants, antique knick-knacks and dozens of paintings on the walls, and has an intimate vibe, like a living room. The service is first class, too. Free-range rabbit, pig and duck are sourced from local organic farms for the Cuban and international cuisine, and the team works with what's available on a daily basis – hence the blackboard menu. Chefs Iván Rodríguez López and Justo Peréz originally worked for Cuba's senior government officials including Fidel; Iván went onto work at top Havana restaurants La Fontana and Castropol before opening the restaurant in 2012. You'll need to reserve for an evening meal; and it's rammed all day on Sundays.

POCKET TIP
Love the food? Head to neighbouring Al Carbón, at street level around the corner, for a popular grill-up.

13 BUENA VISTA CURRY CLUB (BVCC)

Calle Tejadillo 24 e/Cuba y San Ignacio
7862 7379
Mon–Sun 12pm–12am,
live music Tues, Thurs–Sun 8–10pm
[MAP p. 172 B1]

Bollywood meets Buena Vista at this downtown neon-signed Indian joint inside a 19th-century home. A little incongruous, yes, but don't think twice about dining here on account of the soft, garlicky and divine naan bread alone. This homage to Indian cuisine, with a Cuban vibe and live-music nights, is one of the best places to eat in the city. Cigar-smoking Indian Paramjit Chhatwal, who has lived in Cuba for 25 years, dreamt about eating his native country's cuisine until the day he could make his dream come true. Along with his Cuban wife, they sourced a chef from Delhi and import all ingredients. The menu helpfully signals vegetarian dishes and chilli heat for newcomers to the cuisine. While you enjoy your curry New York pianist Tom Placido plays in a jazz trio on Tuesdays, Thursdays, Saturdays and Sundays; an eight-piece Cuban band livens up dinner on Friday nights.

POCKET TIP
If you have no time to sit down while sightseeing, BVCC's El Timbiriche food hatch serves drinks, kebabs and naan bread rolls from 8am–10.30pm.

17

14 5 E/QUINA/

Calle Habana 104 esq
Cuarteles
7860 6295
Mon–Sun 8am–11pm
[MAP p. 171 E3]

Fresh slices of serrano ham, top-notch pizza delivered directly from the wood-fired oven and tasty pasta – all from a tiny corner building that spills out onto a street of tables and parasols. It's popular here, and for good reason. The charcuterie platter is perfect for a quick lunch, as is the moreish 5 Esquinas pizza topped with cheese including blue, goat's and Emmental. The Cuban owners worked for years in Old Havana's top state-run outfit Habaguanex and brought all their know-how to the table to open this sun-splashed cafe with most of its tables on the street. If you've seen *Fast & Furious 8* – this is the place whose tables were wiped out in a tight-alley run by Vin Diesel.

POCKET TIP

Two blocks north, the national Museo de la Música (Calle Capdevila 1 e/ Habana y Aguiar) is due to reopen in 2020.

15 EL FLORIDITA

Calle Obispo 557 esq
Monserrate
7867 1686
Mon–Sun 12pm–12am
[MAP p. 181 B2]

Salmon pink, and flagged by a seductive neon sign, this is where legendary tippler Ernest Hemingway would come after typing up his notes at his base in the **Ambos Mundos Hotel** (Calle Obispo 153) and sink daiquiris especially made for him by bartender Constantino Ribalaigua Vert. The number of daiquiris sold at El Floridita is a secret, I was told. It seems everyone in Havana wants to drink like Hemingway. If it's not your intention, you'll find yourself drawn into the slipstream anyway. The Papa Doble, or Hemingway Daiquiri, pumps double the rum into a glass, removes the sugar and replaces it with grapefruit juice and maraschino liqueur (the original features a double-size daiquiri with lime juice). At CUC$6 a daiquiri, you're not likely to down Hemingway's record of 16, but you can lean in on the bronze bust of the writer for the obligatory shot, admire the gleaming long bar and pounce on a bar stool when it's vacated.

POCKET TIP

Hemingway's ghost lingers at La Bodeguita del Medio, close to the cathedral, but he was never there. It just peddles one of the world's most successful PR campaigns, along with Havana's worst mojito.

19

16 EL DEL FRENTE

Calle O'Reilly 303 e/Habana
y Aguiar
7867 4256
Mon–Sun 12pm–12am
[MAP p. 172 A4]

This wins my vote for Havana's
coolest spot. Hang with
Havana's creatives and young
entrepreneurs at this rooftop
bar and terrace amid the
Edison bulbs, neon and tutti-
frutti coloured metal chairs.
Generous drinks – piña coladas
served in jars, a rollicking
raining geisha (vodka, ginger,
honey and cucumber) – along
with snacks such as tostones
pelotones (ceviche on fried
plantain topped by beetroot
and sesame seed), and the
best citrusy, zesty ceviche
in town, see me pulling up a
chair in here quite frequently.
Owner artist and trained chef
Juan Carlos Imperatori opened
El del Frente in 2015 after the
rocking success of his smaller
gin bar **304 O'Reilly** (directly
opposite on street level). Come
early-ish for nights on the
rooftop; it can be hard to get
a seat by mid-evening. If you
really want that terrace stoop
for the alfresco vibe, call ahead
to reserve.

POCKET TIP
Just around the corner on
Calle Aguiar, there's a mini
neon sign revival (Lafayette,
Jama restaurant, Bar
Eleggua and Helad'oro, *see*
p. 10), bringing a vintage
glow to this street.

SOUTHERN OLD HAVANA

The streets of southern Old Havana are less manicured than those north of Calle Obispo, save for the restored Plaza de San Francisco de Asís (*see* p. 26) and Old Plaza (Plaza Vieja, *see* p. 28). Here you'll find tumbledown streets tall with townhouses and clapped-out hotels-cum-apartment buildings, messy with dogs and cats, playing kids, ankle-breaking potholes, fruit and vegetable sellers, as well as restored pharmacies, museums and under-restoration plazas and churches. The main streets running south of Obispo close to the historic core – Calles San Ignacio, Mercaderes, Oficios – have, in the main, been revived and painted up in candy colours. Turn the corner, and debris and dereliction is in evidence.

Must-visit shops, such as Clandestina (*see* p. 32) and inviting cafes – El Café (*see* p. 38) and El Dandy (*see* p. 39), are pinned to the edges of small, leafy Plaza del Cristo. Way down in the south, close to the monumental central railway station, the former pimp-and-prostitute barrio of San Isidro (*see* p. 30) is emerging as a place to see art, hang, drink and eat. Cuban and foreign street artists have spray-painted homes and buildings along several streets, pivoting around Calle San Isidro.

→ *Dancers at Casa de Africa*

SIGHTS
1. Museo Nacional de la Cerámica Contemporánea Cubana
2. Plaza de San Francisco de Asís
3. Casa de Africa
4. Cámara Oscura
5. Museo de Ron Havana Club
6. San Isidro Distrito de Arte (Art district)

SIGHTS & SHOPPING
7. Taller de Gráfica Serigrafía René Portocarrero

SHOPPING
8. Clandestina
9. Dador
10. Experimental Gallery
11. Casa del Habano
12. Almacenes San José
13. La Marca

EATING
14. El Café
15. El Dandy
16. Creperie Oasis Nelva

EATING & DRINKING
17. Jibaro

1 MUSEO NACIONAL DE LA CERÁMICA CONTEMPORÁNEA CUBANA

Calle Mercaderes 27 esq Calle
Amargura
7801 1130
Tues–Sat 9.30am–5pm,
Sun 9.30am–1pm
[MAP p. 175 D1]

Giant sculptures, quirky
pieces, rude objects and works
by some of Cuba's greatest
artists are found in this
wonderfully engaging ceramic
museum. This place doesn't
ever seem to feature in a list
of top sights so the mansion is
blissfully crowd-free. It houses
the work of Amelia Peláez,
René Portocarrero, Wifredo
Lam, Alfredo Sosabravo,
Beatriz Sala Santacana and
Camagüeyan Martha Jíménez.
My favourite pieces include
the ethereal flaking pages
of an ink-stained book by
Fernando Velázquez Vigil.
Alejandro Cordovés Rodríguez'
miniature animal figures
stuffed with wire for whiskers,
cogs for eyes, tiny lightbulbs
and other discarded electrical
appliances, were fashioned
for a *Frankenstein*'s children
series. Entry is CUC$3.

POCKET TIP

Nearby, the new location of Cuba's museum collection of old and historic buildings, the Museo del Automóvil (El Garaje) has reopened on Calle San Ignacio e/ Amargura y Teniente Rey.

2 PLAZA DE SAN FRANCISCO DE ASÍS

Plaza de San Francisco de Asís
7862 9683
Tues–Sat 10am–5pm, concert
times vary
[MAP p. 175 E2]

The portside, cobblestoned Plaza de San Francisco de Asís, laid out in 1628, faces the Sierra Maestra cruise ship terminal, and an under-construction hotel. The terminal heaved with cruise ship visitors for a few short years until President Trump closed the door on the US cruise ship trade in summer 2019. The towering 1738-built **Basílica Menor y Convento de San Francisco de Asís** is no longer consecrated, after the invading British used it as a weapons store in the 18th century. Today it's famous for its classical music concerts (you'll find info at the door; CUC$10) and a statue outside its door of **El Caballero de Paris** (The Gentleman of Paris), a bronze sculpture of a Spanish down-and-out. Legend dictates that anyone who strokes the statue's beard will have their wishes granted.

POCKET TIP
Facing the basilica tower is the 1909 Lonja del Comercio (Stock Exchange) topped by a statue of the Roman god of commerce, Mercury.

3 CASA DE AFRICA

Calle Obrapía 157 e/calles
Mercaderes y San Ignacio
7861 5798
Tues–Sat 9.30am–5pm,
Sun 9.30am–1pm
[MAP p. 173 D4]

As dusty and as ancient as it appears, this open-sided museum dedicated to African artefacts and influences in Cuba is worth a look. You'll need to hire an English-speaking guide as exhibit labels are in Spanish. Hidden away in a gallery are gifts to Fidel Castro from African leaders: a taxidermied leopard head and skin, and a hanging zebra skin. Wooden masks from Congo and ceremonial decorative masks from Guinea line the museum's walls, while unusual musical instruments including ancient drums line the floors. An altar of the Afro–Cuban religion of Santería (its origins in the Yoruba heartland of western Africa), a Palo Monte (originating in the Bantú-speaking lands of western Africa) shrine tableau, and a table dedicated to Espiritsmo (belief in the benefits or ills of spirits) make it easy to ask the guide questions. It's the only place in downtown to see the striking dance costumes belonging to the secret Abakuá brotherhood (an all-male society with roots in south-east Nigeria).

POCKET TIP

Combine a visit around the Saturday 3pm music billing. Check the cultural calendar posted at the door for all-female folkloric group, Obini Batá. Also, listen out for live *son*, an African–Spanish rooted music played by bands in bars, such as atmospheric La Lluvia del Oro.

4 CÁMARA OSCURA

Cnr Calle Mercaderes &
Teniente Rey
Tues–Sun 9.30am–4.45pm,
Sat–Sun 12pm–5pm
[MAP p. 175 D3]

Hiding in plain sight is this powerful periscope spying on Habaneros daily life from the heights of a corner building in **Plaza Vieja**, via an image created using two lenses and a mirror. It's a pretty cool experience and an excellent place to head early in your Havana visit, as the English-speaking guides explain each of the old city's main buildings while turning the 1.8 metre (5.9 feet) spherical screen 360 degrees around the city seen in miniature. They pepper the talk with snippets of gossip like where Madonna held her 58th birthday party (La Vitrola bar below in the restored 16th-century Plaza Vieja). Get there before 10.30 in the morning to beat the Cuban crowds. Entry is CUC$2.

POCKET TIP
View hunters – the best vista of Old Havana is from the headland next to the statue of Christ in Casablanca across the bay. Photographers note, the best shot is the morning light snap.

POCKET TIP

The real Hershey model town and gardens set up by the American confectioner can still be visited (it's 64 kilometres/40 miles east of Havana); sadly, the electric Hershey train to take you there is out of action.

5 MUSEO DE RON HAVANA CLUB

Avenida del Puerto 262 esq Sol
7861 8051
Mon–Sun 9.30am–5.30pm
Tours in English 11am, 12pm, 2pm, 3pm, 4pm
Bar Mon–Sun 9.30am–12am
[MAP p. 175 F3]

The story of rum built into a beautiful 1780 mansion makes for a double bill in one. You'll get a tour of Cuban rum-making, plus the chance to see the grand dimensions of this 18th-century mansion scented with the smell of molasses and rum. On the first floor, bathed in wonderful light, are some striking mediopunto (half-moon) stained-glass windows. The quality of the tour is dependent on the guide but the highlight is the working model of the Hershey sugar plantation complete with tooting train. You get to smell Cuban molasses – the base ingredient for rum – a knock-out burnt caramel whiff. You'll also see some of the barrels – made from American white oak and used to age whisky in Scotland and Ireland, which are now employed to age Havana Club. After the free tipple at the end, segue to the museum's dark wood street-front **bar** and listen to the live band with a neat rum – now that you've acquired a little spirit know-how. Entry to the museum is CUC$7.

29

6 SAN ISIDRO DISTRITO DE ARTE (ART DISTRICT)

Calle San Isidro 214 e/Picota y Compostela
7864 6713
Mon–Sat 9am–4pm
[MAP p. 178 B3]

For almost 60 years the only painted faces staring out of Havana's walls were those of bearded rebels: Fidel Castro, Raúl Castro and Che Guevara. In the last few years, though, a new breed of painter, armed with sprays and colour cans, has been splashing the paint and creating intriguing and challenging street art. As Amen Perrugorría, son of Cuba's most famous actor Jorge told me, he, his father and his team are trying to create an art district like Miami's Wynwood. The cockpit is found at **Galería Taller Gorría** and new **Restaurant Yarini**. Surrounding streets are flecked with vibrant murals from Cuban and foreign street artists. **Galería El Artista** (Picota 259 e/ San Isidro y Desamparado) showcases young artists. **Bar Jesús María 20** (at the same address) does a stonking daiquiri. There's a February festival in the hood, and regular events; check Instagram – sanisidroda.

POCKET TIP
Near the grand railway station, you'll find Havana's most perfect examples of Art Nouveau – ice-cream coloured buildings in Calle Cárdenas and Calle Cienfuegos; there's also cool street art around these crumbling streets.

7 TALLER DE GRÁFICA ƒERIGRAFÍA RENÉ PORTOCARRERO

Cuba 513 e/Muralla y
Teniente Rey
7801 8354
Mon–Thurs 8am–5pm, Fri
8am–4.30pm
[MAP p. 174 C3]

Step into an antique world of printing presses, slats and wood blocks, and watch staff at work in this cavernous mini-factory – a hotbed of poster making in Havana. The taller works are by designers commissioned by some of the top institutions in the country – Havana Club, the film industry, and theatre – and printed with some wonderful, colourful and collectible avant-garde graphics. An exhibit of posters is always on show at the workshop, which is free to enter. You can also learn silk-screen printing in-house. Don't miss the corner operation printing T-shirts, too. Skip expensive downtown shops selling posters. This place has the best contemporary and historic selection at reasonable prices.

POCKET TIP
Check the website:
red–inkart.com for
upcoming exhibitions
of poster art.

8 CLANDESTINA

403 Calle Villegas e/Teniente
Rey y Muralla
Mon–Sat 10am–8pm, Sun
10am–5pm
[MAP p. 181 C3]

With its cheeky slogans, bold colours and marketing nous, Cuba's first design store is a trailblazer. Graphic designer Idania del Río and her Spanish partner Leire Fernández have navigated the legalities to unveil teasing graphics on T-shirts, totes, badges and posters for visitors wanting to take home a slice of hip Havana from their old town store. The 'actually, I'm in Havana' bags and T-shirts mock the island's lack of wi-fi, stopping you from instantly responding to messages from friends. Clandestina's creations have become must-buy local offerings. Its growing success means it has been able to invite other designers on board, too. Fancy something from the entire range? You can now buy online as Clandestina became the first Cuban fashion brand to sell their wares online. Clandestina's launch parties are pretty damn cool, too.

POCKET TIP

Just across neighbouring Plaza del Cristo is Calle Lamparilla. In Graham Greene' *Our Man in Havana*, vacuum cleaner salesman Wormold's store was at number 37. Its location, when Greene was in town, was a fictional address.

9 DADOR

Calle Amargura 253 e/
Compostela y Habana
Mon–Sat 10am–6pm, Sun
1–6pm
[MAP p. 174 A2]

It's been a while … say
60 years … since high-end
glamour has been plucked
off the hangers in the Cuban
capital, but Dador – which
means the Giver – is changing
that. Three young women who
studied at the School of Design,
opened the unsigned store in
December 2018 with a focus
on limited edition collections.
The material is 100% cotton,
rayon or linen and is sourced in
Cuba or from the States. Their
ambition is to curate three
lines of value and affordability
for women, as well as clothes
worth splashing out on. The
three designers' combined
skills produce fashion that
is durable, comfortable and
works from day through to
night for busy lifestyles. They
also plan to create fashion for
all stages of life, and one-size-
fits-all wearables. Dador's
space in an 1890 tiled-floor
townhouse is alluring, and
changing art pieces can be
seen amid the clothing rails
and dangling jewellery by other
Cuban makers.

10 EXPERIMENTAL GALLERY

Calle Armagura y Aguacate
7867 2548
Mon–Sat 10am–6pm
[MAP p. 181 C2]

A little like a Wunderkammer (cabinet of curiosity), this exposed-brick den of posters, photography and antiques is where to pick up an education on contemporary graphic art and buy an unusual objet d'art. I found a small brass palm tree paperweight with movable fronds here so I'm a fan. Historic revolution posters feature, as do contemporary work by names such as Ares, Xavier Llovet and Zardoyas. Award-winning graphic artist Ares – Aristides Hernández – is famous for his silk-screen printed posters sold at this tiny studio. I bought his well-known 'Cuba PostCastro' poster more than 10 years ago. The best thing about browsing and shopping here is the hugely knowledgeable staff member Yohana who can give you the low-down on all the artists and fill you in on design and poster history, too.

POCKET TIP
If closed, small environments aren't your thing, try the Evocación Tobacco Lounge at the Gran Hotel Manzana Kempinski la Habana (Calle San Rafael e/ Monserrate y Zulueta).

11 CA*S*A DEL HABANO

Hotel Conde de Villanueva
Calle Mercaderes esq
Lamparilla
7862 9293
Mon–Sun 10am–7pm
Cigar class Mon–Sat 10am–4pm
[MAP p. 175 D1]

Let's face it, you can't come to Cuba and not puff on a legendary Cuban cigar. Up on the mezzanine of the grand mansion Hotel Conde de Villanueva, is the most atmospheric of the city's cigar stores – all chairs, books, dark woods and a fug of smoke in a tiny, windowless shop. And Michael Douglas, Naomi Campbell and Paris Hilton who've all passed through, seem to think so, too. Keen to try before you buy? Sign up to the staff's 20-minute (CUC$10) taster class on how to make a Cuban puro (cigar), watching torcedor (roller) Reinaldo at work, while he also explains the different tobacco leaves that are used to craft a Cuban stogie. You'll get a rum and a 'suave' cigar to smoke after 'graduation'.

12 ALMACENE/ /AN JO/É

Avenida del Puerto e/Cuba y
San Ignacio
Mon–Sun 9am–6pm, closed
1st Mon each month
[MAP p. 179 F3]

Short of time and want a
one-stop-market stuffed
with a zillion souvenirs? This
cavernous ex-warehouse on
the water houses hundreds
of stalls. It's not for everyone
as it's large and a tad hassly,
but it's the perfect pit-stop for
those looking to grab a 'Che'
T-shirt, musical instrument,
papier mâché classic car,
baseball bat or cigar humidor.
Most of the art on canvas here,
classed as 'arte feria', is not
to everyone's taste. Seek out
the following from booth 243:
smart handbags, clutches, hats
and shoes made from water
hyacinth. At booth 432 are
D'Brujas who employ eight
women to craft herbal-scented
soaps – they smell beautiful
and are perfect for gifts for
home. If you buy art that is
larger than 30 x 40cm you're
obliged to buy a CUC$2 export
permit from the Registro
Cultural booth in the middle
of the warehouse.

POCKET TIP
Quality art requires an
export certificate. Artists,
or their assistants, will
arrange this for you,
and know the drill.

POCKET TIP

On the same street, the Casa Museo Oswaldo Guayasamín showcases one of the few painted portraits of Fidel – produced by Ecuadorian artist Oswaldo Guayasamín.

13 LA MARCA

Calle Obrapía 108C e/Oficios y Mercaderes
7801 2026
Mon–Sat 11.30am–7pm
[MAP p. 173 E4]

Cultural collective, body art parlour, art venue and all-round centre of Cuban cool, this tiny innovative powerhouse in a manicured street of Old Havana is bursting with ideas and creativity. Most folk know it for the tattoos, and come for one of the designs by the six artists working in the studio, or bring your own (minimum fee CUC$50). Set up by artist Leo Canosa in late 2014, the inking and the art has blossomed. Robertiko Ramos, who studied fashion design, runs the gallery space and organises design and visual art workshops (kids in the neighbourhood can learn about street art). Four visual arts exhibitions are installed each year (but in reality there's a more rapid changeover). Check out its alternative buys, ranging from skating pioneers AmigoSkate products to T-shirts by Estudio 750, and half tee/half traditional Cuban guayabera shirts by Marginalia. Check La Marca's upcoming events, including alternative music nights, on its Facebook page.

14 EL CAFÉ

Calle Armagura 358 e/Villegas
y Aguacate
7861 3817
Mon–Sun 10am–6pm
[MAP p. 181 C2]

This unsigned tiled colonial home on Amargura Street is Havana's best-kept secret. Ridiculously popular with Cuban entrepreneurs, expats and in-the-know tourists, means that you might want to come outside of main meal times to get a seat in the one-roomed space with its mismatched chairs, and long tables. Cuban Nelson Rodríguez Tamayo returned to Cuba to open this caffeine refuge after working in cafes and restaurants in London. As well as its wonderful Cuban Escambray coffee, I always order vegetable juices (beetroot, ginger and pineapple), which are a great detox from cocktails consumed the night before. The sourdough sandwiches, all-day egg and avocado breakfasts, and the fruit and pancake pile-up, are winners. Vegans and vegetarians will want to make their way here – right now!

15 EL DANDY

Calle Teniente Rey (Brasil) 401
e/Villegas, Plaza del Cristo
7867 6463
Mon–Sun 8am–1am
[MAP p. 181 C3]

I make a beeline for El Dandy at lunchtime for its tacos of chicken or pork and people-watching opportunities. With its open windows and doors, luring punters with its ice-blue neon sign and stuffed with tables, chairs, antiques and fabulous photography, it's sometimes hard to break away from the chilled vibe. The bar, with an enormous portrait of a posing dandy, is the picturesque focus, but it's the great-value menu that will keep you coming back – from early morning for the comforting breakfasts to nighttime for the killer classic Cuban cocktails. Try the very perky fulsome signature El Dandy mojito jazzed up with basil. Life-affirming photographs, which beautifully capture the essence of contemporary Havana, are by Swedish photographer Anders Rising, the bar owner's father-in-law. Unfortunately, the eponymous dandy is no longer with us.

POCKET TIP

Nearby La Libertija (Ciclo Ecopapel, Calle Lamparilla 362 e/ Villegas y Aguacate) is a must-visit for handcrafted local ...ods. Created by artist Anáis Triana, ...he focus is on art and crafts made ...m recycled and upcycled materials and handmade paper, and it's a wonderful way to support Cuba's makers.

16 CREPERIE OASIS NELVA

Calle Muralla esq Habana
5293 9758
Mon–Sun 12pm–10pm
[MAP p. 174 B4]

Organic vegetable lovers rejoice! Beside a little plant shop is this small creperie run by Carmen Monteagudo who sources her greens from one of Cuba's most famous organic farms, Finca Marta. You can sit on stacked old tyres or painted boxes amid the hanging plants and tuck into the cheap and tasty crepes. I prefer the savoury – the filling shrimp thermidor (a special), or chicken and mushroom – to the pimped-up sweet ones, such as cocoa and hazelnut layered in syrups. Next up is the owners' crepes and tacos made from yucca flour. Happy hour between 5–7pm is a super popular time to come.

POCKET TIP

If you're travelling in a group, groups can reserve in advance for one of Cuba's best farm-to-fork lunches at Finca Marta (Caimito, Artemisa province). Call 5805 2075.

POCKET TIP

Close by, glimpse the outstanding glorious painted interiors of the Iglesia de la Merced or take a peek at boxers at the Rafael Trejo training gym.

17 JIBARO

Calle Merced 69 e/Cuba y San Ignacio
7860 1725
Mon–Fri 12pm–12am, Sat–Sun 11am–12am.
[MAP p.179 E1]

Famous for its mocktails – think pink ale made from blackberry juice and ginger ale – and now for the street art climbing up its facade, this hole-in-the-wall bar and restaurant is a dream retreat. It was opened by nuclear engineer Diana Figueroa and husband David and is perfect for a pit-stop amid sightseeing. I like the Mula Jibara (ginger ale, coconut horchata and lime), and the rockingly good Michelada Fula (tomato juice, Worcester sauce, lemon juice, pepper, hot sauce, fried tomato, celery salt, topped up with beer). Cocktail and mocktail making is a passion and it was Diana who was chosen to guide HRH Charles and Camilla in the art of mojito making during their 2019 Cuba tour. I like Jibaro's tapas more than the main dishes; try the fish and spinach fritters, malanga fritters with honey, arancini stuffed with mince accompanied by alioli and the ceviche. There's no sign on the door, just the incredibly striking art by street artist Mr Myl, featuring a Jibaro – a dog that runs off into the mountains.

EL PRADO & MALECÓN

In 2016, El Prado avenue was the most Instagrammed spot in the world, as fashion designer Karl Lagerfield paraded his Chanel Resort collection there. The marble-paved promenade points south from Havana's Malecón seawall, an ocean front road which ripples around the Atlantic coast for eight kilometres (five miles). Known affectionately as 'el sofa', the Malecón is where Cubans come to hang, drink, flirt and fish. Salt-bitten buildings are under continuous renovation and during threatening storms the highway is closed. If you're a photographer, and not fussed about getting wet, this is a brilliant time to head down there as the waves roll dramatically over the stone wall.

El Prado, shaded with laurel trees, strikes through an avenue of eclectic facades – a mix of Neoclassical, Arabic, Baroque and Art Deco buildings – and is home to hotels, theatres, shops, palaces and cultural establishments, stretching from the sea south to Parque Central (Central Park). Parque Central (see p. 45) is dominated by a statue of José Martí, poet and mastermind of Cuban independence, and tall royal palms. You'll find yourself here for the Gran Teatro de La Habana Alicia Alonso (see p. 50), hotels, bars, transport and free, clean bathrooms. Head south and the thoroughfare runs past El Capitolio (Capitol Building, see p. 46), and ends with the Hotel Saratoga (host to Beyoncé and Jay-Z in 2013), La Fuente de la India (see p. 51), and Fraternidad Park. Frenchman Jean-Claude Nicolas Forestier was responsible for much of the grand urban boulevards when he cast his expert eye over Havana's layout in the 1920s.

→ *A coco taxi transports tourists along Havana's seaside boulevard, the Malecón, against a backdrop of artwork*

43

1 WALKING EL PRADO

Initially built outside the Old City walls in 1772, the pedestrian boulevard **El Prado** was primped up in the 1920s by French landscape architect Jean-Claude Nicolas Forestier. It is lined with marble benches, lampposts and four bronze lions, which sailed from London in 1920. **Palacio Balaguer**, now hosting Asturias Society restaurants, hides the old **American Club** embellished with 48 coats of arms of American states. Walking north on the left is the 1914 **Palacio de los Matrimonios** (Palace of Marriages). Once the Spanish casino, its ornately decorated main salon hosts weddings and concerts. Further down is the 1908 **Hotel Sevilla** with its Moorish facade and Andalucian tiled lobby. Al Capone lived in room 615 when he visited; Graham Greene fans will know about Room 501 from *Our Man in Havana*. At number 212, the 1915 house of Cuba's second president José Miguel Gómez (now the **Alliance Francaise**) conceals a sparkling stained-glass skylight. Where El Prado meets the Malecón are new hotels: **Iberostar Grand Packard** and **SO/Paseo del Prado La Habana**.

2 PARQUE CENTRAL

Prado e/Neptuno y Obrapía
[MAP p. 181 A2]

With its 1877 marble statue of Cuban hero and mastermind of independence, **José Martí**, this sun-dappled park is a principal pivot of the city. Locals hang out in the little shade provided by the 28 tall palms and small garden shrubbery. On the south side, men's temple veins bulge as they shout at each other in heated arguments – it's all about the baseball results, and known locally as the **Esquina Caliente** (Hot Corner). The park is surrounded by the city's first lodgings, the 1875 **Hotel Inglaterra** and royal blue **Hotel Telégrafo**. There's the aesthetically unappealing but recommended **Hotel Iberostar Parque Central** (with its clean, accessible lavatories), the former newspaper office-turned-lacklustre **Hotel Plaza** and the luxury five-star **Gran Hotel Manzana Kempinski La Habana**, with its rooftop pool and bar, astounding rooftop views and tobacco lounge (see p. 35). **Museo de Bellas Artes** (Universal Section) is in the grand monumental former Centro Asturiano social centre and exhibits paintings from around the world.

POCKET TIP

The park is also the departure point for hop-on hop-off Habana Bus Tour journeys around the city and to the Eastern Beaches (see p. 132).

3 EL CAPITOLIO (CAPITOL BUILDING)

Paseo de Martí
7801 7451
Tours Tues & Thurs–Sat 10am, 11am, 12pm, 2pm, 3pm, 4pm, Wed & Sun 10am, 11am, 12pm
[MAP p. 181 A3]

Impressive on the outside, she's a stunner on the inside. The wedding-cake white Capitol Building has reopened for tours after renovation. Don't miss a tour (buy in advance on the day), where you can goggle at some of the most fabulous interior decor money could buy. Completed in 1928, but not before a Fellini-esque amusement park was erected in the skeleton in a hiatus in the building works, it will eventually be restored as the seat of government. The third largest interior statue in the world – the 49-ton, 22-carat gold leaf-gilded *Statue of the Republic* towers 17 metres (55 feet) and dominates the Hall of the Lost Steps – some 122 metres (400 feet) long. Look out for details, sometimes not pointed out on tours, such as: a highly unusual statue of the devil, the defiant 'Rebel Angel', and the chiselled-out face of fallen-from-favour President Gerardo Machado on one of the bronze bas-relief main doors. Entrance is CUC$10.

POCKET TIP
Virtually unknown to foreigners, highly decorative Café Baco on the third floor of the Fine Arts Museum (Universo Section), between Parque Central and El Floridita, is perfect for refreshments and downtime after your Capitolio visit.

4 MUSEO DE BELLAS ARTES (ARTE CUBANO)

Trocadero e/Monserrate y Zulueta
7862 0140
Tour guide 7863 9484, ext 105
Tues–Sat 9am–5pm, Sun 10am–2pm
[MAP p. 171 D4]

A highlight of a trip to Havana, this extraordinary Rationalist building showcases more than 1000 works of Cuban art spanning the early colonial era (16th century) through to the early 21st century. Reserving a guide (two days in advance in person or by phone) is well worth it. My favourites include the bold colour paintings of Amelia Peláez, the works of Wifredo Lam and Manuel Mendive infused with African religious imagery, the Pop Art paintings of Raúl Martínez and the detailed, verdant canvases of landscape painter Tomás Sánchez. Don't miss the wondrous La Cafedral, a two-metre-high (six feet) cathedral fashioned from Moka pots, a statement on the revered status of coffee in Cuba and created by one of Cuba's top artists Roberto Fabelo in the '90s. Museum entrance is CUC$5; guide service is CUC$2. The museum's small theatre also hosts intimate theatre and music concerts; check the cartelera (calendar) online at bellasartes.co.cu.

POCKET TIP

One block from the museum is the original Sloppy Joe's, fount of alcohol for Prohibition-era American tourists and key location in Graham Greene's book *Our Man in Havana*.

5 MUSEO DE LA REVOLUCIÓN

Calle Refugio 1 e/Zulueta y
Monserrate
7801 5598
Mon–Sun 9.30am–4pm
[MAP p. 171 D3]

No place does guerrilla garb
alongside Tiffany & Co. decor
quite like Cuba. Room after
marble-floored-room tells the
story of the 1959 Revolution,
1961 Bay of Pigs invasion
and 1962 Missile Crisis. But
I'll be honest, a significant
appeal is the building itself.
The 1920 former presidential
palace-turned-museum
with its Baroque dome is
an ode to sumptuous decor,
which is what you'd expect
when Tiffany & Co. were
commissioned to decorate the
interiors. It was designed to
impress, with a graceful central
marble staircase leading to
the gasp-worthy beautiful Hall
of Mirrors. History buffs will
lose themselves in the exhibits
of knives, hats, radios, dolls
and underskirts – to conceal
secret messages – and in a
tour of military hardware,
plus the yacht *Granma* that
brought Fidel to Cuba in 1956
to foment rebellion. Entrance
costs CUC$8 and guided tours
are available. Avoid visiting
on a Monday, as most city
museums are closed, so visitors
descend here.

POCKET TIP

In front of the museum
entrance are remnants
of the Old City walls; in
1863 governors began
tearing them down.

6 GRAN TEATRO DE LA HABANA ALICIA ALONSO

Prado e/San José y San
Rafael blvd
7861 7391
Tues–Sat nine tours 9.30am–
4pm, Sun five tours 9.15am–
12.15pm
[MAP p. 181 A2]

This beautiful building,
billowing with decorative
muses and angels, shimmering
with Italian Carrara marble and
chandeliers, and exquisitely
flood-lit at night, is a must-visit
for both a tour and to see a
performance. The neo-Baroque
building, once the Gallego
Social Centre dating from 1915,
housed an original theatre
that was the blueprint for this
grand version. Its auditorium
has hosted Josephine Baker,
Mikhail Baryshnikov, Enrico
Caruso and Carlos Acosta. It
was lavishly restored in 2016,
in time for President Obama's
historic speech to the Cuban
people. Today, it's the home
of the **National Ballet**.
Look out for performances
by Acosta's talented dance
group, AcostaDanza, too. For
performance information, see
the billboards outside the main
door. Cubans are pretty lax
when it comes to dress code
but the 'no shorts and no flip
flops' rule is strictly enforced.
A tour of the building costs
CUC$5; performance tickets for
foreigners cost CUC$30.

POCKET TIP
Havana's first film was
shown – projected onto
a bed sheet – in a hall
next to the Gran Teatro in
1897 by a French Lumiere
brothers' agent.

7 LA FUENTE DE LA INDIA

Paseo de Martí e/Dragones y Monte
[MAP p. 181 A4]

La Fuente de la India, a graceful fountain ensemble, also known as La Noble Havana, depicts a woman, said to be the wife of Taíno Indian chief Habaguanex. The Taíno were one of several pre-Columbian Indigenous groups living in Cuba. The bare-breasted dame displays Havana's Coat of Arms with one hand: it reveals the city's original forts – Castillo de la Real Fuerza (*see* p. 9), Castillo de los Tres reyes del Morro (*see* p. 127) and La Punta; the key symbolises Havana's position as the gateway to the New World.

8 PRADO ART MARKET

El Prado
Sat–Sun 9am–6pm
[MAP p. 170 C2]

Weekends on the Prado, with the dappled sunlight, artists' easels and stalls, kids on skates, and the odd impromptu music performance, are a perfect time to ramble along the pedestrianised promenade. Take your time, meandering amid the art market stalls as there's also mediocre stuff to wade through. Many artists run their own stalls and they're always available for a chat. Look out for the striking collagraph portraits by Enrique Miralles (Tente); the art of Maykel Felix Guerrero Ramos; the street photography of Diego Fidel Lastre Rodríguez; and the unusual, fun engraved vinyl. There's also copper wire sculpture, origami animals and painted mosaic jewellery. The art is all affordable, bring cash.

POCKET TIP
Swing by Patio de los Artesanos (Calle Obispo) for the interesting vintage graphics-on-wood panels and bookmarks of the artist known as Buby.

9 MEMORIA*

Calle Animas 57 e/Prado y
Zulueta
7862 5153
Mon–Sat 9.30am–5pm
[MAP p. 181 A1]

Revolution drinking glasses,
'50s postcards, old mags,
gorgeous graphics, posters,
vintage casino chips, unusual
books, newspapers, magazines
and historic maps. This tiny
little shop – blink and you'll
miss it – has everything you
could possibly want relating
to the island's culture and
history. Everything is laid
out on tables, shelves, and in
bookcases, mostly with helpful
tags if you want to find maps,
or baseball memorabilia, for
example. But there's more:
Alina and her father Luis, who
run the store, are extremely
helpful, and between them
have an incredible amount of
knowledge. I once wanted a
particular historic poster, and
they offered to track it down,
and keep tabs. The collectibles
aren't particularly cheap here
but they're open to bargaining.

10 NAZDAROVIE

Malecón 25, 2nd floor, e/Prado
y Cárcel
7860 2947
Mon–Sun 12pm–12am
[MAP p. 170 B1]

No other spots in town celebrate the island's Soviet–Cuban legacy but at Nazdarovie, meaning 'Cheers!', they've got fantastic retro posters, the USSR's hammer and sickle flag flying off the balcony, and the real food deal. It has also got the most brilliant terrace on the Malecón for a sundowner. Owned by Ukraine-born Gregory Biniowsky, who, when he arrived in Cuba in 1992, meditated on how Cubans aged 45+ were nostalgic about life studying in the Soviet Union, so he converted his flat into a paladar (private restaurant). Nazdarovie's Russian-born chef cooks up an intensely flavoured beef stroganoff and a perfectly pitched chicken kiev. I recommend its sharing plate – a voyage through the USSR, too. It's a popular spot with Russian embassy staff, and other expats looking for a change from pork and beans.

11 LA TERRAZA

Prado 309 e/Virtudes
7864 1447
Mon–Sun 12pm–12am
[MAP p. 181 A1]

I can't remember how many times I've eaten the tuna fish loin with sesame sauce here. I can't get enough of it. Oh, yeah, and the rosemary-infused pork skewers, grilled octopus and octopus carpaccio, not to mention the superior charred vegetables. The only let-down, in my opinion, is the desserts; they just don't match the quality of the starters and mains. Sit on the peacock chairs on the terrace overlooking Prado and the rooftops of Centro Habana, as the air-conditioned dining room is a bit soulless. You'll need to reserve for dinner if you want to sit on this terrace. This restaurant is inside the former Palacio Balaguer (*see* p. 44) and belongs to the NGO Asturias Society, so profits go to assisting some of the thousands of descendants of Asturians who emigrated to Cuba in the late 19th and early 20th centuries. They have an air-conditioned cigar room for a post-dinner smoke.

CENTRO HAVANA

Appearances are deceptive. This crumbling, salt-whipped district of Spanish-colonial townhouses and stores slumps groundwards with each passing year. Unlike other buffed-up districts of Havana, this mainly residential area has been overlooked in regeneration, apart from its sea-facing facade on the Malecón. Sandwiched between the Prado and Old Havana, and the trafficked Calzada de la Infanta, its grid network of streets is dusty, potholed, sunburnt and bursting with fascinating Habanero life. It also contains the remnants of a Chinatown (including some Cuban–Chinese restaurants and a Chinese arch), that was once only second in size to San Francisco's Chinatown. And behind its closed doors, marble steps and rusty signs are some of the city's most intriguing places to visit.

For photographers, it's a dream, especially places such as Callejón de Hamel (*see* p. 58). In the '50s, this precinct hosted a huge commercial district – along Calle Galiano where big storefronts, neon signs and logos embedded in terrazo pavement can still be seen. From the tobacco perfume wafting out of the Partagás Cigar Factory (*see* p. 64), to the cutting-edge art in Chinatown's Galería Arte Continua (*see* p. 61), to hip-swivelling rumba, restored neon at REX Neon Center (*see* p. 62) and zesty drinks and food at hip-eating haunts such as La Guarida (*see* p. 70) and Michifú (*see* p. 71), this precinct is the place to stroll and flâneur – without limits.

→ *A brightly painted casa particular (B&B) in residential Centro Havana*

1 CALLEJÓN DE HAMEL

Callejón de Hamel, e/Calle
Espada y Calle Aramburu
Mon–Sun 9am–6pm
Rumba Sun 12pm–3pm
[MAP p. 183 F2]

This place will blow your
mind. A small alley wedged
between dishevelled walls
has been transformed
into a colourful homage to
African-origin saints, with
bright street-art wall murals,
hidden shrines and quirky
sculptures fashioned from
the likes of discarded chairs,
bath tubs and typewriters.
It's an extraordinary work of
art, created by artist Salvador
González. But it's not just
perfect fodder for Instagram,
serious business is done here
with the promotion and study
of the African-origin religions:
Santería, Abakuá and Palo
Monte. It's on Sundays when
the place thunders into life
with heart-stopping rumba by
either Rumba Morena or group
Irosso Obbá, and a chance to
witness the three core dances
of this deeply felt secular
dance with vibrant rhythms
springing from Afro–Cuban
instruments and European call
and response songs. Get to the
limited seats by 11am if you
want to sit down; bring water –
you might as well be standing
directly under the Saharan
sun here.

POCKET TIP

Onsite restaurant Barracón is a rip-off. Head instead to nearby cutesy El Cuarto de Tula (San Lázaro 1063) for breakfast or lunch.

2 TEATRO AMÉRICA

Calle Galiano e/Neptuno y
Concordia
7862 5416
Opening hours vary
[MAP p. 180 C2]

Design lovers take heed and
make this your first port of
call in the precinct. This 1941
pale sage and white Rodríguez
Vázquez apartment building
conceals one of Havana's
most glorious theatres on its
first floor. Around a terrazzo
lobby floor featuring Art Deco
symbols of the zodiac rises
a double curved staircase.
Either side are the men's and
women's Art Deco cloakrooms
but it's the ladies with its
pastel palette and retro chairs
that has a spell-binding effect.
If you can't make it past the
doorman to sneak a peak,
book in for a show at the box
office, instead. The auditorium
with its ballooning balconies,
circular iron flourishes and
seductive curves is similar to
New York's Radio City Music
Hall, and is intimate – despite
its 1700 seats. I heard Buena
Vista star Omara Portuondo
sing here in 2012 and I have
never forgotten it.

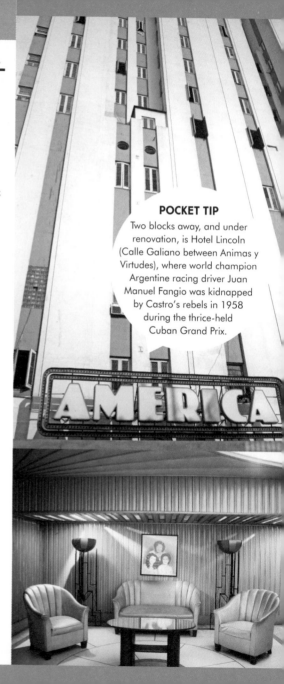

POCKET TIP

Two blocks away, and under
renovation, is Hotel Lincoln
(Calle Galiano between Animas y
Virtudes), where world champion
Argentine racing driver Juan
Manuel Fangio was kidnapped
by Castro's rebels in 1958
during the thrice-held
Cuban Grand Prix.

3 ARTE CONTINUA

Aguila de Oro, Calle Rayo 108,
e/Zanja y Dragones
Tues–Sat 10am–6pm
[MAP p. 180 C3]

French artist JR's huge horizontal image of a local boy on a wall in an urban lot of Chinatown – *Giants, Peeking at the City* – wowed art lovers during Havana's spring 2019 art fair, the Habana Bienal. The high wall forms the side of the old Golden Eagle cinema. Transformed into a cutting-edge art gallery in 2014, it showcases avant-garde art in the old auditorium. Arte Continua is a collective founded by three Italians who run galleries around the world. Recycled paper workshops, music workshops and the like are held in the Chinatown community under the umbrella action Zona Rayo Activo, and are inspired by Italian Michelangelo Pistoletto's Rebirth Embassy/ Third Paradise Project, an ethical approach to balancing the human and natural world equilibrium. On permanent display is a huge domed abdomen *Cuando estoy gestando* (When I am pregnant) by Anish Kapoor, made from plaster of Paris. Launch shows are wildly popular with Habanero millennials. Check social media for events.

POCKET TIP

Wander up Calle Rayo to Calle Salud and admire the fragrant flowers on sale on this street between San Nicolas y Rayo. Further east you'll spy the distinctive giant Chinese Dragon gate heralding the entrance to Chinatown.

61

4 REX NEON CENTER

Blvd San Rafael 161, e/Industria y Amistad
Thurs–Tues 12pm–10pm
[MAP p. 180 C2]

Havana once glowed with multi-coloured neon lights and its theatre district of flashing lights in el Vedado was known as Havana's Broadway. Thanks to a Cuban artist, a New York neon store and a Cuban–American restorer of LA lights, these atmospheric coloured tubes are being repaired and resurrected, bringing a vintage glow back to the city. At the new REX Neon Center, a museum-cum-gallery-cum-workshop-cum-neon boneyard has opened in the shell of the 1938 REX Cinema and adjacent former Cine Duplex. Swing by to see some of the beautifully restored neon, new vintage signs-and-neon work of Kadir López, and the neon boneyard. An art gallery, lecture space, shop, cafe and cinema theatre are all due to open.

POCKET TIP

Two and a half blocks away, behind the Capitolio, is Sía Kará (Calle Barcelona 502 esq Industria), a hidden-behind-the-curtains bar that is perfect for a refreshing lemonade or something stronger out of the sun.

HOTEL
Lincoln
RTUDES 157

HOTEL
Lincoln
VIRTUDES 157
CANDID
LA
VAJILLA

5 PARTAGÁS CIGAR FACTORY

Pollack Bldg
Calle San Carlos e/
Peñalver y Sitios
7873 6056
Mon–Fri 9am–1pm
[MAP p.180 A4]

Fidel Castro's favourite smoke was a Cohiba, created in his honour in 1966. That Cuba, staunch defender of socialism, is the purveyor of one of the world's most recognisable symbols of capitalism, is an irony not lost. To get up close and personal to the rolling of Montecristo, and the like, you'll need to take a tour of the relocated Partagás factory (the famous original behind the Capitolio is closed). Guides lead you up the three floors, with their alternate scents of tobacco and cedar, and past the different cigar-making processes from leaf sorting to rolling and boxing up. Working areas are zoned off, as staff have tried to sell tourists cigars while on the job. Annoyingly, CUC$10 entrance tickets need to be bought at hotel tourism desks in Old Havana. If you can, get here earlier than the 11am tour, as it becomes very crowded. Bags must be stashed in lockers and no photography is allowed.

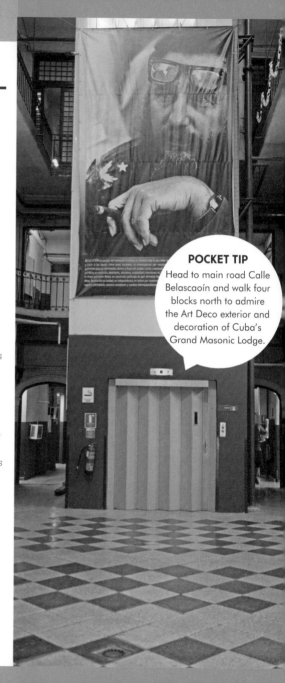

POCKET TIP
Head to main road Calle Belascaoín and walk four blocks north to admire the Art Deco exterior and decoration of Cuba's Grand Masonic Lodge.

6 ESTUDIO 50

Calle Lugareño e/Carlos III y
Almendares
5266 7043
Various opening hours
facebook.com/estudio50cuba
[MAP p. 183 E4]

Art space, party hangout
and competition venue. This
vast former mirror factory
is the hottest industrial
ruin in Havana. In 2019, the
multipurpose space hosted
a rockin' magazine party,
the hugely varied art exhibit
'Illness has a Colour' for
the Habana Bienal (Havana
Biennial) art fair and a music
and DJ HAPE party (keep your
eyes peeled for HAPE's super-
cool parties where foreigners –
but not Cubans – pay to party).
In summer 2019, it was the
stage for Conbac, Havana's
first craft cocktail competition.
Check its Facebook page for
upcoming events.

7 CAPICÚA

San Lázaro 55 e/Cárcel y
Genios
Mon–Sun 10am–6pm
[MAP p. 170 B1]

Fruity jewellery, bold coloured
belt bags and rainbow
African-print jewellery. It's
light, bright and seductive at
Capicúa – meaning head and
tail in Catalan, a new store
collective in a city with new
fashion stores that you can
count on one hand. Brainchild
of designer Laila Chaaban, it
not only features her clothes,
garments and tunics – one-
off pieces made from fabric
trimmings – but those of other
designers, too. There's René
Pedroso's jewellery line called
Click (think perky electrical
switch earrings); cloth Jibaro
bags imprinted with motifs;
and designer illustrations and
vibrant Joy Color jewellery that
includes desirable – almost
edible – acrylic geometric
watermelon pendants, for
example, by designer Yamile
Salomón Infante. You'll also
find colourful African print
waist or shoulder bug bags
by Wasasa; Katy Ocaña
scoops up Wasasa's leftover
material and creates necklaces
fashioned with buttons and
earrings, too.

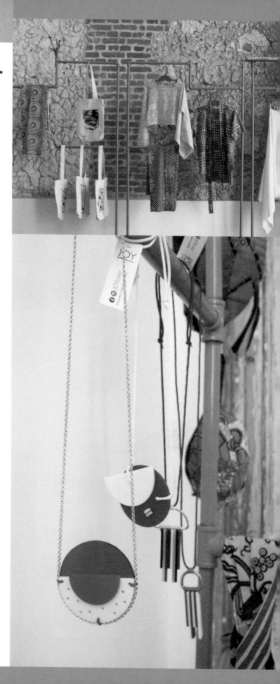

8 CAFÉ ARCANGEL

Calle Concordia 57 e/Galiano
& Aguila
7867 7495
Mon–Sun 8am–6pm
[MAP p. 180 C2]

In a scruffy zone of Centro Havana, with few other inviting options, Café Arcangel stands out for eclectic decor, great coffee and good-value food. Breakfast outside of B&Bs in Cuba is a new thing but if you're staying in Central Havana this should be your first port of call. Before you even get to the food you'll be enticed by its shabby chic louvred front doors, knick-knack decor of ballet shoes, old telephones, lamps, crockery, clapboard and Laurel & Hardy films spooling through an ancient TV. Sit down at Singer sewing machines converted into tables with ceramic tiled tops and tuck in. Coffee comes from the Escambray Mountains and is ground in-house; fruit, vegetables and honey come from organic sources. Its filling Havana Lunch is a bargain – rice, fried plantain, fried egg, ice-cream coffee, water or juice all for CUC$5. Arcangel is co-owned by María Elena and son Joao, a professor of classical ballet who, fascinated by angels, curated the angel wings theme, and also trained to be a barista in Colombia.

9 SAN CRISTÓBAL

Calle San Rafael 469 e/Lealtad
y Campanario
7860 1705
Mon–Sat 12pm–12am
[MAP p. 180 B2]

Known as 'the restaurant
where the Obamas ate', the
then US president and his
family were handed top advice,
as this place is slick, boasts
fascinating interior decor, is
run by a chef who greets diners
personally and, it goes without
saying, serves great Cuban–
Creole food. Carlos, always in
his chef's apron, converted
his colonial townhouse into
a restaurant–museum full
of Russian dolls, statues,
records, painting, furniture
and a religious shrine, all set
against the beautiful tenor of
a dozen chiming clocks. Opt
for the mixed starter platter –
Mezedes de la Casa – a meze
of dishes like malanga fritters,
tortilla and a ceviche of
aubergine. Then ask if they've
got langostinos and order them
laced in lashings of garlic.
Their flan is pretty darn fine,
too. At the end of every meal,
you're served a trago (drink) of
rum and given a cigar. There's
no better treatment elsewhere.
Reserve a month in advance to
eat in 'Salon Obama'.

POCKET TIP
Just one block north
is Patio El Jelengue de
Areito (San Miguel 410 e/
Campanario y Lealtad). Go
for the mobbed matinees;
Fridays are for rumba
5–8pm (CUC$5).

10 SALCHIPIZZA

Calzada de Infanta 562 e/Valle
y Zapata
5281 8792
Tues–Sat 9am–4pm
[MAP p. 183 E3]

Michelin stars and modest bakeries are not common partners in cuisine, but at this unusual Havana bakery you'll find this unique combination. I met chef Alberto González Ceballos a few years ago through a friend who started buying his rye bread. It doesn't sound particularly unusual but tasteless Cuban 'bread' flakes are like wood chippings so baking decent bread on the island is a revered art. Alberto was head cook at a Michelin-starred restaurant in Italy before returning to Cuba in 2013 and opening Salchipizza on a wide, broken-down avenue on the gritty edge of Centro. Sit down for breakfast under his glass-bottled ceiling. I relish the fried duck and quail eggs, gluten-free bread, dried fruit bread, and rye bread accompanied by beetroot butter, fine herb butter and white truffle. A serving of ham cured for 90 days with herbs had me begging for more. Alberto's breakfast is CUC$7 per person; more can be ordered for a lunch of 3–5 dishes for CUC$15–18 per person; reservations are essential for the 12pm–4pm lunch slot.

11 LA GUARIDA

Calle Concordia 418 e/
Gervasio y Escobar
7866 9047
Mon–Sun 12pm–4pm & 7pm–
12am. Bar Mon–Sun 6pm–2am.
[MAP p. 180 A2]

Come for the glamour, the
shattered beauty of the
building, the flapping drying
bed sheets on the first floor,
the New Cuban food and the
rooftop bar. This is Havana's
most famous restaurant, which
shot to fame when it was
featured in the 1994 Cuban
movie, *Fresa y Chocolate*
(Strawberry & Chocolate) by
directors Tomás Gutiérrez
Alea and Juan Carlos Tabío.
After a dinner of delicious
roasted suckling pig bathed
in a honey orange reduction
(ask for a cute balcony table
if possible), climb the spiral
staircase to the roof bar where
young architects have fitted
outsized picture frames to the
terrace. Sit on one of the inbuilt
seats and enjoy this chic spot
for an evening drink. Every
celebrity who has ever been to
Havana has come to dine; and
Rihanna posed on the marble
steps for her Annie Leibovitz
Vanity Fair shoot in 2015. Artist
Esterio Segura's film prop
religious statuary graces one
of the salons. Reserve well in
advance, especially for dinner.

12 MICHIFÚ

Calle Concordia 368 e/Escobar
7862 4869
Mon–Sun 12pm–12am
[MAP p. 180 B2]

A killer passionfruit cocktail alfresco on a steamy Havana night? Yes, please! You enter past the swanky rope and cinematic bar and you should aim for a spot on the interior patio amid the plants, banquette and colourful cushions. Michifú is part-restaurant and part-bar. It all has a hint of a sun-kissed Marrakesh alfresco roof terrace to it. Live piano music defines the night from 9–11pm. The chalked-up menu offers good-value dishes, such as Basque tuna in ratatouille and pollo vasco (strips of chicken in ratatouille with malanga and pumpkin purée). As you asked – michifú is a homemade cheap drink made from firewater and chunks of pineapple, popular in the '80s. A revived version with additional secret ingredients is on offer here – just ask at the bar. The dynamic folks behind this cool Centro Habana bar first opened popular Siá Kará behind the Capitol in Old Havana but moved away to inject more life into Centro Habana. They've succeeded and we're grateful.

13 EL BATAZO

Calle Belascoaín 211 e/
Neptuno y Concordia
7864 5029
Opening hours vary
[MAP p. 180 A2]

This down-to-earth little music venue and community project is filled with locals having a good time amid the eye-popping sculptures and antique emporium at the door. A Christ's crucifix fashioned from steel rods had me transfixed. Pinned to the wall, it joins a bank of old typewriters and a giant steel rod bat sculpture inside a roofless gutted old supermarket. Artist Vladimir Martínez Avila and Lenin Abreu Molina have opened this community project with dual purpose: a place of entertainment and a school to train kids and teens so they can pass exams to gain entry into Cuba's prestigious school of arts. The centre houses a bar (alcohol is not sold between 5 and 7pm), cafe, good-value restaurant (Creole food is served after 3pm) and stage. Recent 8pm shows have featured Cuban actor Bárbaro Marín; singer María Victoria Rodríguez; son music ensemble Septeto Nacional; and Habana Salsa. Wednesday nights usually feature Drag. All proceeds support the cultural projects at the centre. Music events cost CUC$5 for foreigners.

14 MALECÓN 663

Malecón 663 e/Gervasio y
Belascaoín
7860 1459
Rooftop terrace Mon–Sun
6–11pm
[MAP p. 180 A1]

This labour of love on the
Malecón is Havana's first
artisan-created boutique
hotel and it enjoys awesome
sunset views over the rippling
ocean promenade. Come for
the views of the Atlantic,
the passing glinting-finned
Chevys cruising by in the sun,
the drinks, the DJs and the
cool factor. Run by Orlandito
Mengual, conga player for
hit timba band Charanga
Habanera and his French wife
Sandra, they called up all their
designer and architect friends
to fashion a work of art that
is constantly being updated.
It's a hive of activity in the
lobby-cum-living-room, with a
bar during the daytime (happy
hour is 5–8pm), while at night
the vibe moves to the rooftop
terrace for their sundown
*No te bañes en el Malecón
(Don't bathe on the Malecón)*.
Come for jazz on Thursdays
with Marcos Morales Quintet;
Fridays with singer De.R.O.I
(#therhythmofindia); and
Sundays for chill-out sunset
sessions with DJ Landeep.
Occasional Kundalini yoga and
Thai massage are held on the
roof by Agata Yoga, too.

EL VEDADO LA RAMPA & AROUND

West of Centro Havana is El Vedado. Most visitors don't stay in this precinct, preferring the busy streets of the historic old city to leafy, broad-avenued El Vedado, but this barrio – with its palaces like pastries, gated villas, Art Deco towers and 1950s hotels – offers plenty if you want to understand 21st-century Havana. It's where I always stay in a Cuban homestay or a new-generation boutique hotel. Built off the back of Cuba's world record-breaking 19th-century sugar boom, the island's sugar rich invested their profits and built a precinct that even today has few rivals to its architectural wealth in all of Latin America.

This guidebook divides this large precinct in two: firstly the club, cinema and hotel district around Avenida 23 (La Rampa) and west to the broad Avenue of Presidents (Calle G), known for its statues of Latin American leaders. Secondly, further west around the leafy Paseo avenue, Plaza de la Revolución (see El Vedado Paseo, Plaza de la Revolución & around chapter, p. 90) and on to the Almendares River.

→ Havana's iconic Hotel Nacional, and tunnels used during the 1962 Cuban missile crisis

SIGHTS
1. Self-guided walk
2. Hotel Nacional tour/ Missile Crisis tunnels
3. Museo Napoleónico
4. University of Havana museums
5. Estudio Figueroa-Vives

EATING
6. Coppelia
7. Grados
8. Awesome Dumplings
9. Mediterráneo

DRINKING
10. Centro Cultural Bertolt Brecht (No sé lo digas a Nadie)
11. La Zorra y el Cuervo

1 ∫ELF-GUIDED WALK

This area will take you back in time to 1950s Havana when President Fulgencio Batista's hotel law offered ridiculous incentives to builders. The mafia, hung up on converting Havana into the Las Vegas of the Caribbean, built the **Hotel Riviera** (*see* p. 100), and the **Hotel Capri** and casino in 1956 (Calle N e/19 y 21). Its rooftop pool featured in the avant-garde opening long-shot of the iconic 1964 Soviet–Cuban movie *Soy Cuba*. The Capri was also where Michael Corleone stayed in Francis Ford Coppola's *The Godfather Part II*, although the actual movie wasn't shot here; but a scene from Graham Greene's *Our Man in Havana* movie was filmed here in 1959. Head one block north on Calle M and at number 17 is the towering sage green and dirty cream 1956 **Focsa** building, the largest in Cuba with 400 apartments. If the 33rd-floor bar **La Torre** is open, the views of the city are unrivalled. On the corner of La Rampa and Calle L rears the **Hotel Tryp Habana Libre**, a US $24 million investment by Hilton in 1958. The almost-original Hilton trademark Trader Vic's tiki restaurant (today, **El Polinesio**) is in the basement.

POCKET TIP

When Castro and his rebel army marched into Havana in 1959, they set up their HQ in Hotel Habana Libre. Fidel's room can be visited by making a reservation at 8.30am with the concierge one day before you plan to visit.

2 HOTEL NACIONAL TOUR/MISSILE CRISIS TUNNELS

Calle 21 y O
7836 3564
Tours Mon–Sat 10am
[MAP p. 183 E1]

In 1946 American mobsters sat down here to a dinner of roast manatee and roast flamingo amid the refinery and the chandeliers. It's not hard to imagine this in the imposing hotel which has sat on a bluff overlooking the Atlantic for 90 years. The storied hotel, built like a pseudo-castle with a magical lobby decked out in Andalucian tiles, has hosted a glitterati of world leaders and starlets – everyone from Winston Churchill to Rita Hayworth. Get the juicy lowdown on a tour, which takes you up to floors with rooms marked with plaques for VIP visitors, up one of the hotel towers with panoramic views, into the Hall of Fame, and down to the gardens to see cannons and a subterranean bunker and tunnels, used by Fidel's government during the 1962 Cuban Missile Crisis. Wondering about a stay? Book a room on the upper VIP floors. Failing that, come for drinks, the tour and the historic glamour. Tours are free to hotel guests, or CUC$5, with a drink included.

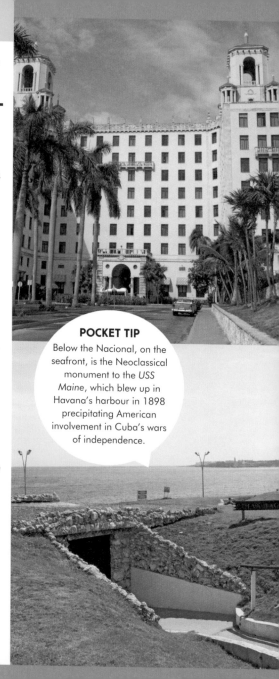

POCKET TIP

Below the Nacional, on the seafront, is the Neoclassical monument to the *USS Maine*, which blew up in Havana's harbour in 1898 precipitating American involvement in Cuba's wars of independence.

POCKET TIP
Cool off with an ice-cream or top-rated Burner Brothers' cake in the air-conditioned cool of Monte Freddo's smart parlour behind the museum (Calle San Rafael 1209 e/Ronda y Mazón).

3 MUSEO NAPOLEÓNICO

Calle San Miguel 1159 esq Ronda
7879 1412
Tues–Sat 9.30am–5pm, Sun 9.30am–12.30pm
[MAP p. 183 E3]

Napoleon's locks of hair and other parts of his corpse may be hidden somewhere on the island, according to the *Financial Times*' Latin America correspondent John Paul Rathbone. He wrote as much in his fascinating 2010 book *The Sugar King of Havana* about sugar baron Julio Lobo who acquired the largest collection of Napoleonic memorabilia outside of Europe. The museum is housed in a sumptuous Florentine mansion, all marble and stained glass, which belonged to Orestes Ferrara, a Neapolitan who fought for the Cubans in the 1898 Spanish–American War. Bonaparte's last doctor, Corsican Francesco Antommarchi retired to Cuba. He created three death masks of Napoleon, one of which, in bronze, sits on a bedside table next to Napoleon's bed on the second floor. Don't miss the 19th-century carved coconut used for gunpowder, take a peek inside the marble and mahogany library and sit in the garden for quiet contemplation. Entrance is CUC$3.

4 UNIVERSITY OF HAVANA MUSEUMS

Calle L e/Ronda y Jovellar
7831 3750/7879 3488
Mon–Fri 9am–12pm, 1.30–4pm
[MAP p.183 E3]

POCKET TIP

Look for the bronze Alma Mater statue at the top of the 88 steps of the university – made in 1919 by Czech artist Mario Korbel.

Taxidermied whales hang from the ceiling and stuffed small animals and birds pose in Victorian-era cabinets in this true Cuban Wunderkammer (cabinet of curiosity). The **Museo de Historia Natural Felipe Poey** is hidden amid the lofty columns of Havana's university buildings and is an absolute cracker of a museum, and one of my favourites in the city. It's dusty, dark and worn, and there's talk of renovation but I hope it's not touched. It's a learning curve, too, if you want to get a close-up of the entire constellation of Cuba's animals, birds, fish, fossils and molluscs. Cuban naturalist Felipe Poey, an authority on Cuban fish, established the museum in 1842, making it the oldest in Havana. Entrance costs just CUC$1. Upstairs, the highlight at the **Museo Antrópologico Montané** (Anthropology Museum) is the wooden Taíno tobacco idol, a one-eyed anthropomorphic sculpture, brought from eastern Guantánamo province. The university, founded in 1728, and in its current location since 1902, is a peaceful place to wander or read; there's also a small cafe.

5 ESTUDIO FIGUEROA-VIVES

Calle 21 no 303 apt 2 e/H e l
7832 6332
Mon–Fri 10.30am–4.30pm
[MAP p. 182 C2]

This is the home-studio of the photographer José A Figueroa and his curator wife Cristina Vives. Figueroa began his career by working with the famous Cuban snapper Alberto Korda (a fashion photographer turned documenter of Fidel Castro's Revolution who captured the iconic image of Che Guevara taken at a funeral in 1960). They host regular collective exhibitions with the support of the neighbouring Norwegian Embassy. Opening nights for shows are mega popular with Cuban cultural stars and fans.

POCKET TIP
Two blocks north is UNEAC (Calle 17 corner of Calle H), HQ of the National Union of Writers and Artists of Cuba. Check the cultural calendar, at the railings, for music events at this mansion.

MILLONARIOS DE LA REVOLUCIÓN

LAS MARIANAS

POCKET TIP

A few blocks north is the Tribuna Antimperialista, a public square used for gatherings, protests, and concerts since 2000. It faces the 1952-built newly revived US Embassy.

6 COPPELIA

Calle 23 (La Rampa), cnr Calle L
Tues–Sun 10am–9.15pm
[MAP p. 183 D2]

A spaceship structure, hovering on one of the city's most famous junctions, was once the premier ice-cream parlour in Havana. There are better places for flavoursome scoops but Coppelia is affordable for all Cubans who will queue for hours for cheap ice-cream at this hallowed place. Flavours are down from about 26 in 1966 to about 10 to 14 today, but that doesn't deter the hundreds who form lines on Calle 23 and around the block. For more expensive ice-cream and no lines, head to the pink and brown air-conditioned cafe on the premises, although this misses the point of the shared experience. Fidel's secretary and confidant Celia Sánchez christened the architect-designed helado (ice-cream) emporium Coppelia after her favourite ballet. Today, its government-owned franchises are found all over the country. Coppelia is also famous for its appearance in Cuba's only movie to get a foreign film nomination at the Oscars, *Fresa y Chocolate* (*Strawberry & Chocolate*), where protagonists David and Diego meet for a bowl of the chilled stuff.

POCKET TIP
Vietnam's former communist leader, Ho Chi Minh, apparently welcomed a Cubana plane once a week carrying Coppelia ice-cream just for him!

7 GRADOS

Calle E 562 e/23 y 25
7833 7882
Wed–Sun 12.30pm–3.30pm,
7–10.30pm
[MAP p. 182 C3]

It's the chef, the food, the ideas, and the old-school format that does it for me. Mentored at Michelin-starred Atrio in Spain's Extramadura, Raulito Bazuka, born of a Cuban mother and Uruguayan guerrilla father, has opened this small paladar (private restaurant) in his mother's prettily tiled front room and terrace. He has mirrored the way these private Mom and Pop places were established in Cuba in the '90s. My favourite dish is the beautifully tender medallions of lamb laced in the herby, seedy Pru, a fermented herbal brew originating in Cuba's far east. I also fail to resist his stonking Baked Alaska every time. Bazuka read the diaries of historic Cuban leaders to bring to the table a revived version of these dishes. He's ever the out-of-the-box inventor, so after his clever, avant-garde Matrix-themed food and performance event during 2019's Habana Bienal art fair, he's now creating his own-brand drinks, and challenging culinary norms through a new venture – Salón de Protocolo.

POCKET TIP

Just around the corner on Calle 23, between E and F, Bar EFE with its urban Berlin club vibe ramps up the night with DJs mixing electronic tunes, jazz and other on-trend music.

8 AWESOME DUMPLINGS

Calle 13 no. 160 e/L y K
5887 1108
Mon–Sun 11am–11pm
[MAP p. 182 C1]

In a city not known for its Asian food, and with only traces of its Chinese legacy remaining, this no-frills, no-fuss diner is the real-deal. So much so that the Chinese owner and chef, Eliu, doesn't speak Spanish or English and employs a Chinese-speaking Cuban to interpret. Eliu from Tianjin imports all her ingredients from China. The specialty is those awesome dumplings. I like the steamed pork, shrimps and egg varieties. Servings are super generous, so much so that you could order one between two; they come with pots of garlic and chilli to accompany. It's mega popular with the Chinese expat community so you know you're on the right track. Service is a tad on the slow side so don't come in a rush. Dozens of other dishes are available, too.

POCKET TIP
Nearby El Apartamento (Calle 15 313 esq H, apto 3), owned by young Cuban collector Christian Gundín, is a sought-after venue for Cuba's most exciting contemporary artists.

9 MEDITERRÁNEO

Calle 13, 406 entre F y G
7832 4894
Mon–Sun 12pm–12am
[MAP p. 182 B2]

Fresh goat's cheese in Havana?
Yes, please. This successful
private restaurant, headed
by a Sardinian chef, has its
operation really worked out.
Its cooperative finca (organic
farm cooperative), just outside
of Havana, has free-roaming
goats and pigs, and terraces
of organic vegetables and
herbs supplying half of the
restaurant's food. The fish
comes from the Gulf of
Batabanó, off the south coast
of the island, where the wife of
the restaurant owner comes
from a family of fishermen.
The fresh-off-the-boat fish is
never frozen and defrosted.
Whether you opt for the
alfresco terrace for dinner or
the air-conditioned cool for
lunch in the blue and white
house off broad Avenue G,
it's all delicious and made
by chef Luigi Fiori. I nearly
always order the perfectly
pitched gazpacho with crispy
croutons, and I love the ravioli
in cheese sauce with truffles.
This restaurant is just west of
Avenida de los Presidentes.
To tour and dine at their
Vista Hermosa Farm, check
the restaurant's website
(medhavana.com).

POCKET TIP
The distinctive grey Deco-
ish building, Casa de las
Américas (Calle 3 esq G),
wind-whipped by the sea at
the northern end of Avenue
of the Presidents holds
rotating exhibitions in
its art gallery.

10 CENTRO CULTURAL BERTOLT BRECHT (NO ʃE LO DIGAʃ A NADIE)

Calle 13 esq I
7830 1354/7832 9359
Wed–Sun 10pm–late
[MAP p. 182 C1]

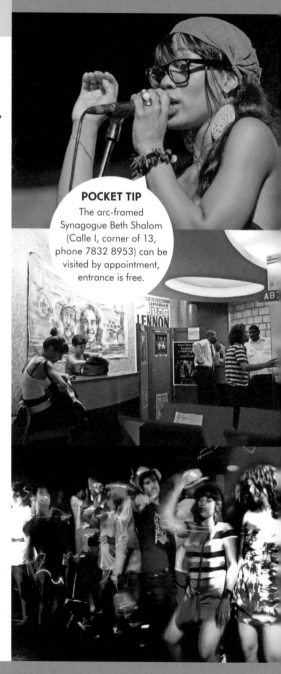

This basement den is one of the city's hippest haunts. Music fans sip cocktails and beers at the '50s-vibe curved bar before moving into the intimate low-lit venue. You'll hear the likes of pianist Robertico Carcassés and his experimental band Interactivo on Wednesday nights, or star songstress Telmary and her group Habana Sana, who mixes up hip hop, Afro-Cuban rhythms, funk, timba, jazz and more. Tables curve around the edge but most folks are thronged in the centre of the floor. You'll need to call or swing by to see the line-up and there's a CUC$5 entry fee for foreigners. The unusual building also features a first-floor **cafetería** and **theatre** for avant-garde performances; at the back sits the **Synagogue Beth Shalom** (*see* pocket tip). The reason for this unusual configuration is that the building was built in 1953 for the Beth Shalom community; it was divided in 1981 and part-sold to the Ministry of Culture; the synagogue is what remains for the community.

POCKET TIP

The arc-framed Synagogue Beth Shalom (Calle I, corner of 13, phone 7832 8953) can be visited by appointment, entrance is free.

11 LA ZORRA Y EL CUERVO

Calle 23 e/N y O
7833 2402
Mon–Sun 10pm–2am
[MAP p. 183 E2]

Step through the imitation red London-style telephone box door and down into this cosy smoky basement for nightly jazz. Well-known jazz pianist Roberto Fonseca often takes to the stage at the 'Fox and the Crow' a few times a month. Look out also for percussionist Ruy López-Nussa from the talented López–Nussa family, and gifted pianist Aldo López Gavilán. The monthly line-up is posted in the window of the telephone box; entrance is CUC$10 with two national drinks provided.

POCKET TIP
The International Jazz Plaza Festival takes place across Havana venues every January.

89

EL VEDADO PASEO, PLAZA DE LA REVOLUCIÓN & AROUND

The broad, tree-lined streets of graceful old mansions, porticoed villas, Art Deco apartments and '50s buildings, continues to unfurl west from the Avenue of the Presidents (*see* El Vedado La Rampa & around chapter, p. 74) towards Paseo and the Almendares River. You'll spend your days finding artsy bars, apartments-turned-art galleries, paladares (private restaurants) in manicured mansions, tiled cafes, craftsmen in garages, restored 1950s hotel gems and music haunts in low-lit basements and skyscrapers. It's also Havana's theatre land with its vibrant array of theatres, dance studios, cinemas and salsa clubs, where you can catch world-class cultural shows at show-stopping bargain prices.

El Vedado's tree-lined streets also feature some of the city's most curious attractions: the monumental marble city of the dead, the Necrópolis de Colón (Christopher Columbus Necropolis, *see* p. 94), the Fábrica de Arte Cubano (Cuban Arts Factory, *see* p. 93) and the jungle hideaway of Jardines de la Tropical (*see* p. 98).

➹ *Cubans wait for a bus outside the mural-splashed Cuban Arts Factory*

1 MUSEO NACIONAL DE ARTES DECORATIVAS (MUSEUM OF DECORATIVE ARTS)

Calle 17 esq E
7830 9848
Tues–Sat 9.30am–4pm
[MAP p. 182 B2]

Want to know how ridiculously rich high-society Habaneros were in the early 20th century? Then this outstanding mansion is a jaw-dropper. Sugar baron José Gómez-Mena Vila moved into the property in the 1920s; the family home was later inherited by his widowed sister María Luisa Gómez-Mena Vila (Countess of Revilla de Camargo). The grandiose home is stuffed with some 33,000 antiques, including 18th-century French carpets, ebony sculptures, Maison Jansen furnishings, and a 17th-century hunting horn emblazoned with hunters and animals. The glass collection is impressive, too – René Lalique vases and Tiffany & Co. bowls and vases. Don't miss the Art Deco pink marble bathroom. Today, the museum is a popular spot for 15-year-old girls (Quinceañeras), making their debut in society, to have their photographs taken on the glorious staircase. Mansion entry is CUC$5.

POCKET TIP
Show-stopping exhibits by a constellation of Cuba's top artists are often held at Galería Habana (Calle Línea 460 e/ E and F) a small, state-run gallery.

2 FÁBRICA DE ARTE CUBANO (CUBAN ARTS FACTORY)

26 St, cnr 11th St
Thurs–Sun 8pm–2am (Jan–Apr,
June–Aug & Oct–Dec)
[MAP p. 185 E2]

The brainchild of a rock musician X Alfonso and the Ministry of Culture, the Cuban Arts Factory continues to rock Havana's cultural life. La Fábrica, a converted peanut oil factory, embraces music, cinema, fashion, bars, theatre, art and photography across several floors and cavernous corners. With multiple highlights billed over its long weekend openings, it draws young Cubans, hipster visitors, temba (over age 40) couples, Havana's farándula (movers and shakers) and all types in between. With one entrance fee for all, drinks bought marked on cards (with payment on exit), and the chance to rub shoulders with fashion models, musicians and famous artists, it's way too easy to hang until dawn. **Tierra** (see p. 103) serves 20 global platters from across the world, and a new alfresco VIP lounge (ostensibly for a puff on a Cuban cigar) rests on the girders of stacked shipping containers encouraging night caps until the 2am closing time. Entrance to the Fábrica is CUC$2.

POCKET TIP

The wildly colourful murals on the walls of the Fábrica de Arte Cubano buildings – *Se Permuta* – were a Cuban–Brazilian collaboration led by Cuban graphic artist David Alfonso.

3 NECRÓPOLIS DE CRISTÓBAL COLÓN (CHRISTOPHER COLUMBUS NECROPOLIS)

Calle Zapata y Calle 12
7830 4517
Mon–Sun 8am–5pm
[MAP p. 185 F2]

This city of the dead, the largest communion of marble angels in Latin America, is so expansive, its 21 avenues are numbered for navigation. I like to spend a couple of hours here – for photography, the Art Deco tombs, the curious sculptures and the quiet. I recommend hiring a guide (tips appreciated) to get the low-down on the most important burials and structures and then explore on your own with the official map (CUC$1). My favourite tombs are the Art Deco Baró family pantheon, designed by René Lalique and patterned with windows engraved with roses, and striking doors featuring two exquisite carved winged angels. The shimmering golden mosaic image by famous Cuban artist René Portocarrero adorns the interior of the Raúl de Zárraga vault; and the sleeping dog at the foot of the Jeannette Ryder sepulchre is worth seeing. Carry water before you go in – it's hot and there's no shade. Entrance is CUC$5.

POCKET TIP
After a trip to the cemetery, snack or lunch on the burgers at nearby Café hoy como ayer (Calle 12 554 e/ 23 y 25).

POCKET TIP

A few blocks from the cemetery, check out the Cuban Cinematographic Institute's office (Calle 23 1155 e/10 y 12), entirely papered in classic Cuban film posters.

4 CASA DE LA AMISTAD

Paseo between Calles 17 y 19
7833 1922
Mon–Sun 9am–5pm (house),
Mon–Sun 9am–10pm (cafe)
[MAP p. 182 B3]

Juan Pedro Baró loved his
wife so much he named a rose
after her, built a magnificent
Art Deco tomb (*see* p. 94) for
her mortal remains in 1930,
and built this dusty pink
mansion for her in 1926. Today
the Italian Renaissance villa
houses the Cuban Institute for
Friendship with the Peoples,
but you can wander in, peek
at the Art Deco Primavera
dining room, marble staircase,
exquisite stained-glass on
the first floor, and buy what's
probably the cheapest drink
in this precinct, sitting under
the eye-popping geometric
dome of the **cafe**. When Baró
met dazzling Catalina Lasa,
she was married and at the
time there were no divorce
laws in Cuba. They eloped to
France, appealed (successfully)
in 1917 for the Pope to anul
Lasa's marriage to husband
Pedro Estévez, and returned
to build one of the most
magnificent homes in Havana.
It's CUC$2 entry, CUC$5 for
photos. Weekend evenings
are devoted to live salsa in the
patio (CUC$4) and popular rock
nights on Sundays (CUC$2).

POCKET TIP

The swanky Pablo González
de Mendoza y Pedroso home
(Paseo at Calle 15), one
block north, now the British
Ambassador's residence, has a
ridiculously glamorous indoor
Roman Bath overlooked by
a marble statue
of Aphrodite.

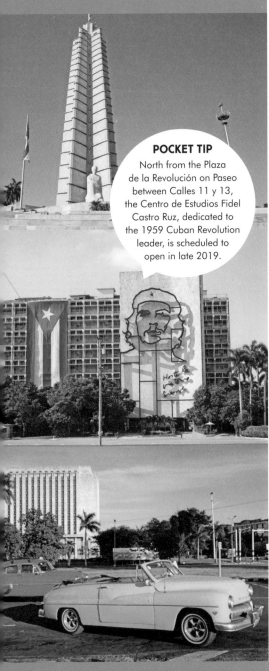

5 PLAZA DE LA REVOLUCIÓN

Paseo cnr Avenida de la
Independencia
Memorial José Martí Mon–Fri
9.30am–4pm, Sat 9.30–
12.30pm
7859 2347
[MAP p. 187 B2]

This monumental plaza has
seen it all. It's where popes
have shaken hands in historic
meetings with Fidel Castro,
May Day Parades march by,
and where a huge homage to
Fidel was held the week of his
death in 2016. Come for the
history, and the great photo
opportunities. Everyone wants
a shot of the Che Guevara
silhouette sculpture cast in
iron pinned to the Ministry
of the Interior, and the newer
neighbouring iron portrait
of Revolution leader Camilo
Cienfuegos that hangs on the
Communications Ministry.
Views of the city from the
109 metre-high (357 feet)
marble tower, the highest
point in Havana, belong to
the **Memorial José Martí**
(access CUC$5) and are worth
the elevator ride. The outsized
marble statue of poet, journalist
and national independence
hero José Martí, sits at its base.

POCKET TIP

North from the Plaza
de la Revolución on Paseo
between Calles 11 y 13,
the Centro de Estudios Fidel
Castro Ruz, dedicated to
the 1959 Cuban Revolution
leader, is scheduled to
open in late 2019.

6 JARDINE/ DE LA TROPICAL

Calle Rizo y Final, enter from
Avenida 51
7886 1767
[MAP p. 186 C1]

A jungle eyrie with a whiff of a *Hansel and Gretel* gingerbread home, buried amid the lush banyan trees of Havana's park, is one of my favourite escapes from the city. La Tropical Brewery built this riverside fantasy playground for their workers in 1904 in a corner of the 21 hectares (51 acres) of the Metropolitan Park. The trees are draped in so much flowing verdant vine that they resemble evening gowns. Socialites once gathered to dance under the open-sided Dream Hall, its ceiling studded with colourful starfish made from cement; they'd then wander into the Moorish mini Alhambra Palace to hear the flutter of piano tunes. Beer is still served from the back of the cutesy chapel. The structures including steps, towers and grottos – built like tree trunks and branches to purposefully blend with the tangle of trees – underwent renovation for Havana's 500th birthday in November 2019. Occasional events are still held here; check social media for news.

POCKET TIP
HAPE Collective, breaking musical boundaries, organises pop-up parties in random places across Havana, including at the Almendares palace. See its Facebook page for events.

7 BELVIEW ARTCAFÉ

Calle 6 412, cnr 19th St
7832 5429
Tues–Thurs 9am–6pm, Fri–Sun
9am–11pm
[MAP p. 182 A4, 185 F1]

I love this cafe. From the sharp
snapshots of Fidel Castro
and Cuban life on the peach
Melba walls, to the ridiculously
cool 1957 baby blue Chevvy
Bel Air-turned sofa, great-
value food and relaxed vibe.
Few people spent as much
time in the presence of Fidel
Castro as German Sven
Creutzmann whose camera
has captured Cuba on film
since 1988. Come to while
away a few hours admiring
Sven's incredible shots, the
retro vinyl player, jukebox and
vintage radio, while devouring
the fresh, homemade food
that is cooked and prepared
at the time of ordering. Their
mamey milkshake is awesome!
Crepes are really good, too.

POCKET TIP

One block north is Parque
ohn Lennon named after the
famous Beatle, whose brass
figure sits on a park bench.
The Yellow Submarine music
enue, known for bands who
play covers, is found on the
park corner, too.

8 BEIRUT SHAWARMA

Calle 1ra 237 Apto A e/A y B
7831 5883
Mon–Sun 12pm–12am
[MAP p. 182 A2]

Opening a Lebanese restaurant in Havana might have been considered a gamble. But it has paid off brilliantly for the Syrian owner who lives in Cuba. This no-frills and no-views spot is packed because it delivers very tasty Arabic food in generous portions at great value with speedy and friendly service. I nearly always order a lunchtime Combo Beirut – a platter of pita bread, hummus, vegetables, chicken shawarma, falafel, a great, smoky baba ganoush and kebbe. Main course dishes are much more generous than most other restaurants in Havana. You can get food delivered to your accommodation, too – a newish concept in Havana – for a minimum CUC$15 order.

POCKET TIP

Close by on Paseo and the Malecón stands the time-capsuled Hotel Riviera, with its coffin-shaped pool. Owned by American mobster Meyer Lansky it opened in 1957 with Ginger Rogers singing her way through the opening night.

9 CUBA LIBRO

Calle 24 no 30 esq Calle 19
Mon–Sat 10am–7pm
[MAP p. 185 E2]

Heaven in a hammock. Finding somewhere to truly chill with good coffee is hard in Havana, but at this leafy residential address with alfresco patio tables, hammocks, and art and sculpture thrown into the mix, is a neat little Anglo–Cuban corner. Welcoming all stripes and with a menu accessible to most Cuban pockets, means coffee and juice won't bust the bank. The conversation flows with the locals who can afford to drink here, and you can pick up local news and browse the reading material. It's run by American Conner Gorry, who has lived in Cuba since 2002, as an ethical and socially responsible business. Books are for sale, references are to read on the spot, and if you can bring books in to donate, they'll be warmly received. Check the cafe's Facebook page for cultural events.

10 CAMINO AL SOL

Calle 3ra 363 e/Paseo y 2
7832 1861
Mon–Sat 10am–10pm
[MAP p.168 C2]

In a country hooked on pork, rice and beans, this small, modest cafe is a godsend. Fresh, homemade moringa pasta, beetroot juice, refreshing gazpacho and filling pumpkin tart are offered as part of very affordable daily offerings chalked up on a board at the cafe entrance. Yunalvis Hernández, a former engineer-turned chef who became a vegetarian 12 years ago, immersed herself in four years' kitchen training and opened this ground floor cafe in 2013. Order at the counter before sitting down at the tables surrounded by pistachio-green walls, white chairs, plants and botanical-themed photos; or browse the deli counter for take-away treats. Yunalvis' produce comes from her own garden plot and the agromercados (points of sale where Cubans sell fruit and vegetables) around the city.

POCKET TIP
Camino al Sol sits behind the towering Melia Cohiba hotel. There's an official taxi rank here, plus unofficial taxis parked in the lot opposite; always negotiate prices.

11 TIERRA

26 St, cnr 11th St
5565 2621
Thurs–Sun 8.30pm–1.30am
[MAP p. 185 E2]

There's something very refreshing about Tierra – a funky alfresco bar and a culinary roam through 20 global dishes, served up in converted shipping containers inside Havana's buzzing Fábrica de Arte Cubano (Cuban Arts Factory, *see* p. 93). Kick off with one of the city's best mojitos – the rocking mojito especial made with Ron Añejo Especial and cava. Then dine in or out starting with the salty empanadas, followed by the British platter: fish and chips served up on a bread board with a couple of dipping sauces. Tierra is run by Hector Higuera, who has years of experience running private restaurants and events in Havana. It's worth reserving a table on Friday and Saturday nights to skip the long line to get into the building.

12 LA CASA DE LA BOMBILLA VERDE

Calle 11 905 e/6 y 8
5848 1331
Tues–Sun 5pm–1am
[MAP p. 185 F1]

The only way to detect the House of the Green Light Bulb is by the faint green glow struggling to make an impact above a door in a dimly lit street of grand residences. Once inside, the vibe is warm and inviting at this hidden, intimate music joint that welcomes singer-songwriters, especially young trovadors (singers), to take to the floor several nights a week. The mixed crowd of multi-generational cool Habaneros gather on bar stools, and cosy around shared tables to sip great-value mojitos amid contemporary art, a vintage white Frigidaire, and a comic-strip lined bathroom. Check its Facebook page for events, and if Santa Clara's Roly Berrío is playing, don't miss it.

13 *SÁBADO* DE LA RUMBA

El Palenque, Calle 4 e/5 y
Calzada
7830 3060
Sat 3–5.30pm
[MAP p. 168 C2]

Want to witness some
seriously nifty footwork?
Swing by an El Vedado patio
on Saturday afternoons to
soak up a flourish of dancers
from the Conjunto Folkórico
Nacional who expertly whirl
about during a full percussion
fest. Get there early, grab a
beer from the bar and claim
a front-row seat. Bring a hat,
too, as the patio is not entirely
shaded. The virtuoso costumed
dancers expertly demonstrate
the trio of rumba – yambú
(a slow partnership dance),
more popular guaguancó (a
frenetic, flirtatious partnership
dance), and the columbía
(solo male energetic dance).
You'll also see orisha dances
(moves honouring the saints
of the Afro–Cuban religion of
Santería), country dances, son,
cha cha cha, and the Mambo.
Ring Thursdays to find out
if stellar groups such as Los
Muñequitos de Matanzas,
or Cutumba from Santiago,
are rolling up to perform.
Entry is CUC$5.

105

14 EL COCINERO

Calle 26 e/11 y 13
7832 2355
Mon–Sun 12pm–12am (terrace)
[MAP p. 185 E2]

Of all the bars in all Havana, El Cocinero boasts wow factor. You'll enter via a corkscrew staircase up a towering chimney that opens out into an alfresco terrace filled with Havana's most beautiful design and people. Havana's beauty is really on show here under the canopy amid the white tables, reproduced Panton chairs, clinking of glasses, and the fantastic, colourful iron-lettering art work by Cuban artist Damian Aquiles. The rooftop bar is part of the same converted peanut oil factory complex as the Fábrica de Arte Cubano (Cuban Arts Factory, *see* p. 93), and is the perfect spot to begin the evening with cocktails before hopping next door to the FAC. There's no cocktail menu; waiters will tell you what's available when they come to your table.

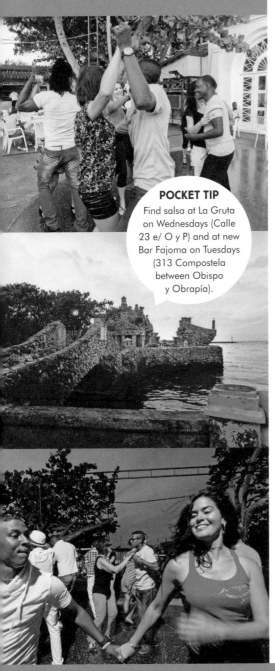

15 SALSA 1830

Malecón y Calle 20
7838 3090
Tues & Thurs–Sun 8pm–1am
[MAP p. 185 E1]

Havana's well-loved salsa club, known locally as milocho, stumps up the big guys from time to time, such as Havana d'Primera. Don't miss them. There's nothing better than dancing salsa alfresco in the gardens to a live, full scale all-singing-all-dancing timba band. If you're a woman on your own, I find this place more comfortable to dance, than say La Gruta, in the La Rampa neighbourhood. Cuban men who invite you to dance may want you to stick with them but dance with as many partners as you like. Proyecto de la Rueda Casino group run regular salsa nights on Tuesdays, Thursdays, Saturdays and Sundays. There's a cloakroom, small bar and seating at the 2019-revamped venue. Entrance is CUC$5.

POCKET TIP

Find salsa at La Gruta on Wednesdays (Calle 23 e/ O y P) and at new Bar Fajoma on Tuesdays (313 Compostela between Obispo y Obrapía).

16 CAFÉ MADRIGAL

Calle 17 809 altos e/Calle 2 y 4
7831 2433
Tues–Sun 6pm–2am
[MAP p. 182 A3]

Café Madrigal was Havana's first private bar. This top floor, artfully decorated space, in a handsome two-storey home, works beautifully for its top-notch cocktails and sun-splashed terrace. It's also blissfully free of blasting reggaeton, which means it's a peaceful place for drinking and chatting with friends in otherwise noisy Havana. Owned by Rafael Rosales, filmmaker and assistant director of Cuban movie *Madrigal*, it attracts an arty crowd. Customers sit at the scattered tables between the exposed brick walls adorned with large-scale portraits on canvas by Cuban artist Javier Guerra, and old cameras, radios and movie-making tools. Madrigal's mojitos are strong; the lovely, light daiquiri is perfectly pitched.

POCKET TIP

Walk up and down nearby Calle 2, a leafy street of fine wedding-cake mansions to see what old and new money could buy. There are new-generation private boutique hotels and the vast mansion housing the Ministry of Culture.

PLAYA &
BEYOND

Upmarket Miramar in the Playa district with its pastel porticoed mansions and top restaurants unfurls west of the Almendares River, along grand avenues lined with leafy trees and flame trees, which drip their dazzling blood orange petals around here in May. Quinta Avenida (Fifth Avenue, see p. 112), lined with Neoclassical mansions and Art Deco wonders – now all embassies, government offices, or foreign company headquarters – rolls out some eight kilometres (5 miles) west. Beyond is the retro palace of cabaret, the Tropicana Cabaret (see p. 123), and the intriguing, beautiful Instituto Superior de Arte (ISA School of Art, see p. 114), on the grounds of the former Country Club where anti-bourgeois Fidel Castro and Che Guevara played that most bourgeois of games, golf. The mosaic wonderland – Estudio Taller José Fuster (Fusterlandia, see p. 115) – that patterns the fishermen's community of Jaimanitas is further west.

Some of Havana's top dining experiences are to be found in this precinct, such as Otramanera (see p. 118), as well as top music and bar haunts, such as El Diablo Tun Tun (see p. 122).

→ *Cuban artist José Fuster has transformed his neighbourhood with decorative tiles. Here, Cuba's 'mejor amigo', the late Venezuelan President Hugo Chávez, is granted a whole street corner.*

El Mejor Amigo

1 QUINTA AVENIDA (FIFTH AVENUE)

Apart from some wonderful places to eat, the main reason to walk Quinta Avenida is to spy the grand homes of Cuba's former elite. The eyesore, always coming into view, is the colossal robot-like 1985 tower of the Russian Embassy. If you walk its perimeter, spy cameras twist and turn and follow you around! The straight-as-an-arrow four-lane avenue begins at the marble **Fuente de las Américas** (fountain). You'll pass the **Memorial de la Denuncia** (corner of Calle 14) with high-tech information displays, and weaponry exhibits detailing how Fidel Castro's Cuba confronted its enemies. Music fans can tour **Casa Museo Compay Segundo** (Calle 22 103 e/ 3ra y 1ra), home of one of Cuba's most famous singers, Compay Segundo who shot to fame with the launch of Ry Cooder's *Buena Vista Social Club* son music album. Fans will want to take a look around and see where the star's discs and trophies hang. Compay Segundo lived here from 1998 until his death in 2003 (his tomb can be seen at Santa Ifigenia Cemetery in Santiago de Cuba).

POCKET TIP

Heading north to the sea, beyond First Avenue, you'll find local hangout, Playita 16 (Calle 16), a limestone platform with a couple of benches from where hardy locals take morning dips and scuba-divers clamber into the water.

2 INSTITUTO SUPERIOR DE ARTE (ISA, SCHOOL OF ART)

904 Calle 120 between 9 Av y 23 Av, Cubanacán
7208 0704
[MAP p. 189 F3]

Brick tubes that twist and turn like fallopian tubes, a fountain in the shape of a vagina, and an abandoned dance auditorium. This is Cuba's School of Arts. It's supposedly off-limits to visitors now, but it's worth getting a gander, if only from the perimeter fences. Or else time your visit to coincide with the month-long Habana Bienal art fair, as shows and performance are always held in the extensive grounds, which once belonged to the pre-Revolution Country Club. Fidel Castro turfed the golfers off the club grounds and donated the site to one of the first commissioned architectural works of his new government. Architects, Cuban Ricardo Porro, and Italians Vittorio Garatti and Roberto Gottardi built five schools of fine arts, dance, music, ballet and theatre between 1962–5. The unfinished domed school of ballet, an auditorium of beautiful Catalan vaults, is set to be restored by the Carlos Acosta Foundation.

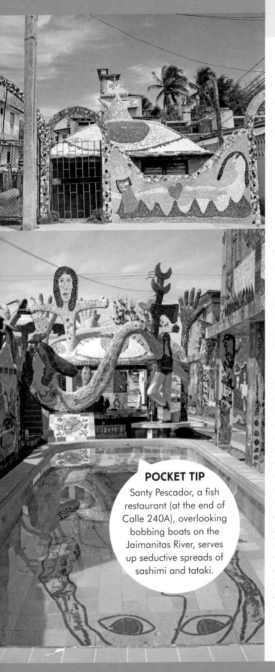

3 ESTUDIO TALLER JOSÉ FUSTER (FUSTERLANDIA)

Calle 226 y Av 3ra-A,
Jaimanitas
7271 2932
Mon–Sun 9am–5pm
[MAP p. 188 A2]

Not even Barcelona's famous architect, Antoni Gaudí, known for his Catalan Modernism and mosaic work, had such free reign as Cuban artist José Fuster, whose only limit is his imagination. With the consent of his neighbours, he's enhanced streets surrounding his home in trencadí (broken mosaic decoration). The homes on the main street, Calle 226, leading off Quinta Avenida (Fifth Avenue) to his house, are covered in shiny mosaic murals with bold images of animals, birds and political figures (think Che Guevara and Hugo Chávez). Even the artist's swimming pool in the grounds of his house is a work of decoration; and a bus shelter out on Fifth Avenue itself (*see* p. 112) gets the Fuster treatment, too. There's quite a buzz there, with a bar and souvenir shops close to Fuster's home. You can buy Fuster tiles and other collectibles from a small shop inside the artist's home. The artist is not usually seen now but his son manages the project.

POCKET TIP

Santy Pescador, a fish restaurant (at the end of Calle 240A), overlooking bobbing boats on the Jaimanitas River, serves up seductive spreads of sashimi and tataki.

115

4 ſEIS ſEIſ

Calle 44 No.4109 e/41 y 38,
Kohly
5290 8177
Mon–Fri 10am–5pm, weekends
by appointment
[MAP p. 186 B1]

The only space in Havana
with a special focus on Cuba's
contemporary photographers,
this studio (in the Kohly
district) is worth seeking
out. Look out for the soulful
black and white documentary
images of life in Cuba by Raúl
Cañibano, the historic Cuban
Revolution work of Ernesto
Fernández, who accompanied
Fidel to the Bay of Pigs – his
image of Che cutting cane is
featured on Cuba's three peso
(CUP) bill. Fernández' son
Ernesto Fernández Zalacaín
is a multimedia artist and
incorporates photography into
his work. Prolific photographer
René Peña's black and white
work often challenges social
and accepted norms. Other
exciting artists to look out
for are Adriana Arronte and
Angel Delgado, who works
outside of Cuba after a hugely
controversial art performance
in 1990 that gave him a prison
sentence. Seis Seis is run by
Cuban art curator, Sandra
Contreras, who brings years
of Cuban gallery experience
to the project.

POCKET TIP

One of Cuba's most
celebrated contemporary
multimedia artists, Sandra
Ramos, has her home-
studio nearby (Calle 49,
2847 e/ 28 y 34). Ring
7209 6381 to make an
appointment.

5 ALMA

Calle 18 314 e/3ra y 5ta,
Miramar
5535 5828
Mon–Sat 10am–6.30pm, by
appointment other times
[MAP p. 184 C2]

When you walk into Alma you instantly know you'll find that birthday gift or unique Cuban-made piece to take home. Housed in a light-filled glass-fronted mini mansion, Alex Oppmann has scoured Cuba for beautiful and interesting hand-crafted products. From the woodworkers of distant Baracoa to the jewellery makers of Pinar del Río and prolific designers in Havana, her curated collection of artisanal gifts will make you wish you'd left more room in your suitcase. Affordable marble paper notebooks, vinyl upcycled into bags, leather clutches in silver embellished with Cuban slogans, and cocoa butter in beautiful wooden pots from the steamy eastern cocoa belt, are all easily packed. Some products sold see a portion of profits sent to an animal protection group; and folks from an old people's home make crafts, with their profits returned directly to the home. Alex also runs free-of-charge workshops for adults and children (check Alma's social media).

POCKET TIP

Hail a classic Cuban American car (almendrón taxi) on Third Avenue for 20CUP or CUC$1 back to downtown, or head to Hecho en Casa (see p. 119) for lunch or dinner.

6 OTRAMANERA

Calle 35 no. 1810 e/20 y 41,
Miramar
7203 8315
Tues–Sat 12.30pm–11pm
[MAP p. 185 D3]

My favourite place in Havana if I want to splash the cash. The food, the service and the ambience are exquisite at this Cuban–Spanish owned elegant restaurant backdropped by a Korean artist's abstract paintings. Spanish sommelier Alvaro Díez Fernández and art graduate Amy Torralbas Lorenzo unveiled their restaurant in 2014, fashioned out of Amy's family's 1950's home, in the upmarket district of Playa. Chef Dayron Avila, who has worked in some of the city's best restaurants, turns out refined delicious dishes with a Mediterranean base and a Cuban touch: fish fritters are lightly fried, delicate, and served in a mini chrome French fries basket along with garlicky sauce. The perfectly pitched and presented tuna tataki with citrus reduction and rocket leaves is what I usually order; and the velvety guava panacottas, and moreish mamey fruit creme brûlée are a hit. Aranjuez-born Alvaro studied to be a sommelier in Girona under sommelier-professors who'd worked at Spain's ground-breaking three-star Michelin restaurant El Bulli.

POCKET TIP

Come for a meal before or after the music at the Casa de la Música, just up the road.

118

POCKET TIP

Just two blocks east is Espacios (Calle 10 e/ Calle 31 y Av 5), an art-decorated alfresco bar in a mansion patio that is famous for its party nights and musical events.

7 CASA-RESTAURANTE-DELICATESSEN HECHO EN CASA

Calle 14 511 e/5ta y 7ta
7202 5392
Mon–Sat 12pm–10pm
[MAP p. 185 D2]

This small paladar (private restaurant) is a little secret. Chef Alina María Menéndez Lamas' heads out every day to shop for fresh ingredients at organic gardens. From the vegetarian moussaka layered with aubergine, cheese, tomato, carrots and herbs, to the tomato soup criss-crossed with chives and served with goat's cheese on toast, to the intensely rich ice-cream made from Baracoa cocoa, you could really spend the entire day ordering passionately prepared, homemade food. Best, then, for those of us who want to gorge at leisure at this little under-the-radar restaurant. The daily changing menu is chalked up on a board on the ground floor and the upstairs dining room is light and bright. Vegans, vegetarians and anyone with food allergies are catered for; get in touch one day in advance. A new deli – for take-away meals, pestos, goat's cheese and other goodies – opened in autumn 2019.

8 AMIR SHISHA

115 Calle 40A e/1ra y 3ra,
Miramar
7206 3443
Mon–Sun 12pm–12am
[MAP p. 184 A3]

The Korean owner of this upmarket restaurant has embraced Lebanese food in her restaurant, alongside her native Korean cuisine. It serves only organic halal lamb and chicken from the kitchen, and dishes are fragrant, delicious and crowd-pleasing. My go-to is the scented chicken shawarma. On hot days, the interior air-conditioned cool of the restaurant with its floor-to-ceiling glass windows is a must. But the lovely swanky garden, with its relaxed seating under a canopy of bamboo terracing is the place to hang once the sting of the sun subsides. Wednesdays and Thursdays see a violinist and pianist play from 8–10.30pm, while Saturdays make way for Arabic dancing with a live Arabic instrument ensemble from 8–11pm. Fancy a hookah? Flavours come in apple, grape, melon and mint.

9 LA COCINA DE LILLIAM

Calle 48 1311 e/13 y 15,
Miramar
7209 6514
Tues–Sat 12pm–3pm & 7–11pm
[MAP p. 184 B4]

After 25 years, La Cocina de Lilliam remains one of the top dining experiences in the capital. Lilliam Domínguez worked in fashion and interior design before turning her hand to the kitchen. She opened her garden paladar (private restaurant) in 1994 when Cuba's government permitted small family-run restaurants during the 'Special Period' – a euphemism for when Cuba found itself in economic dire straits after losing Russian subsidies following the collapse of the Soviet Union. Lilliam's homemade herb bread, swordfish en papillote infused with aromatic basil, coriander, hierba buena mint and chilli, and her flavoured ice-cream made from condensed milk – think basil flecked with hierba buena mint and almond – draw diners time and time again. You'll love her artfully decorated garden, bathed in soft tropical light, and open-sided restaurant.

POCKET TIP

Just 30 minutes west of Havana in Caimito, is garden oasis Finca Tungasuk, where a four-course farm-to-table organic lunch, cooked by Paris-trained chef Annabelle, is a culinary highlight of your trip. Farm volunteers are welcome, too.

10 EL DIABLO TUN TUN

Casa de la Música, Calle
20 3308 esq 35, Miramar
7202 6147
Tues–Sun 5pm–late, check
event listings
facebook.com/tuntundiablo
[MAP p. 185 D3]

Every Thursday at 5pm,
Cubans of all generations pack
into the piano-bar above the
city's main Casa de la Música
to hear the rhyme, rhythm,
cheek and savvy humour
of novissima trovador Ray
Fernández. Fernández has
been bringing the house down
for years following his popular
success when he played to
crowds on Havana's Malecón.
Get to Tun Tun early to secure
seats and a table or just pack
in with everyone else, toting
beers and rums, to listen
and chuckle at this popular
matinee. Guitar-strumming
Fernandez's amusing and
pointed lyrics are adored by
his Cuban fans.

POCKET TIP

Fancy a light bite before or
after the show? Cabin-style
Café Bahía (Calle 41 1402
entre 14 y 18), with its
generous portions of zesty
ceviche, and flavour-laced
juices is a few minutes'
walk away.

11 TROPICANA CABARET

72 e/45 y Línea del Ferrocarril, Marianao
7267 0110
Mon–Sun 8.30pm–12.30am, show begins at 10pm
[MAP p. 186 A4]

Fancy a trip back to the '50s? A 'Night Under the Stars' at the neon-decorated Tropicana delivers. The irony though, is that Castro tried to ban what lingered of the louche 1950s: the casinos, prostitution and the mafia, but this extraordinary show celebrating the era – all feathers, sequins, and outlandish headpieces – is a regular sell-out. This cabaret, one of the most famous in the world in the '50s, even boasted its own plane – the Cabaret in the Sky – that flew back and forth from Miami. If photography's your game, bag the top tickets with seating next to the stage. Buy tickets on the day from hotel tourism bureaux; if it rains the show is moved inside to the Arcos de Cristal hall. Tickets are CUC$75 for seats at the rear of the auditorium; CUC$85 for the middle; CUC$95 to be seated next to the stage. Prices include a quarter of a bottle of Havana Club rum per person, a soda, dried fruit and a welcome drink. There is an additional charge for camera use.

ACROSS THE HARBOUR & THE SOUTH

The under-explored eastern side of the Bay of Havana is filled with castles, rockets and religious heritage. It's a fascinating precinct for history buffs to explore and those looking for a more local and laid-back experience.

It's frequently reached by taking a taxi or bus under a 733-metre (2404 feet) tunnel at the tip of Old Havana, which emerges next to Castillo de los Tres Reyes del Morro and its lighthouse (see p. 127). Unfurling south of El Morro, is the vast flank of the Fortaleza San Carlos de La Cabaña (see p. 126). More atmospheric, and cheaper, is to take the ferry along with the locals to Casablanca (where the castle and fortress can be reached by climbing a road above the town which emerges at the giant marble statue of El Cristo), and to Regla (see p. 129), an untouristy fishing town. To the south is Museo Hemingway (Finca La Vigía, see p. 130), the hilltop villa home of American novelist Ernest Hemingway, which receives a steady flow of pilgrims to where he lived, wrote and drank for 20 years.

→ *The Three Kings Castle of el Morro and lighthouse dominate the entrance to Havana's ample bay*

1 FORTALEZA SAN CARLOS DE LA CABAÑA

Habana del Este
Mon–Sun 10am–10pm
[MAP p. 177 A2]

King Carlos III of Spain was said to have told his governors in Havana that the cost of erecting the 700-metre-long (2296 feet) La Cabaña fortress was so vast he ought to be able to see it through his spyglass from Spain! It was, in fact, already redundant by the time it was built – a year after the British took Havana in 1762. It's 20th-century history is less palatable – it was where prisoners were executed under Che Guevara's orders. Che's command post is now a separate **museum** (CUC$6), but the fortress contains an informative Che museum within its grounds. The fortress itself is vast and shadeless. What is worthwhile are the morning views of the Old City from the nearby **El Cristo statue**; and the rockets lined up behind La Cabaña from the 1962 Missile Crisis. The **cañonazo** – the nightly theatrically staged firing of cannon to mark the closing of the old city walls –takes place at 9pm in the fortress grounds. The fortress costs CUC$6 before 6pm; after 6pm it's CUC$8; guide service costs CUC$2.

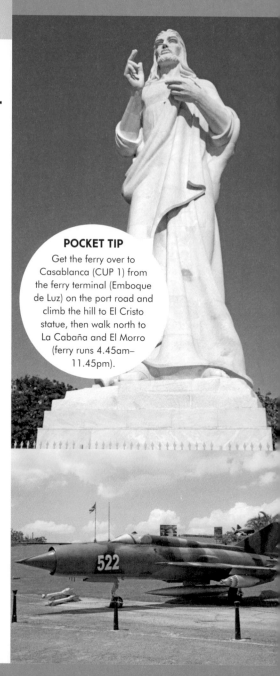

POCKET TIP
Get the ferry over to Casablanca (CUP 1) from the ferry terminal (Emboque de Luz) on the port road and climb the hill to El Cristo statue, then walk north to La Cabaña and El Morro (ferry runs 4.45am–11.45pm).

2 CASTILLO DE LOS TRES REYES DEL MORRO

Habana del Este
7791 1223, ext 124
Mon–Sun 10am–6pm
[MAP p. 176 A1]

The British bombarded El Morro from the sea in 1762 and were able to overrun the unprotected headland, mortally wound the Spanish governor and plant the British flag. Today, the **ramparts** – built between 1589 and 1640 – can be climbed, there's a small memorial to the fatally injured governor, a chapel, and an exhibit on the Italian builders of the castle. The **lighthouse**, now an iconic symbol of Havana, swivels light across the bay and can be climbed (all 117 steps) at 10am, 11.30am, 2.30pm and 5pm. The ramparts cost CUC$6, guide service is CUC$2 and the lighthouse is CUC$6 extra.

127

3 GUANABACOA

Museo Municipal de
Guanabacoa
Calle Martí 108 esq Versalles
7797 9117
Tues–Sat 9.45am–4.30pm
[MAP p. 191 B3]

A town, founded in 1554, and steeped in the Afro–Cuban religions of Santería, Palo Monte and Abakuá, is also home to Jewish cemeteries, a great little museum, and a riotous festival. The **Museo Municipal de Guanabacoa**, a huge mid-19th-century home, with stained-glass windows above rounded arches and a patio, houses fascinating displays of Cuba's African-origin religions. If you're lucky, you'll catch a folkloric dance performance by Grupo Olurún. The museum also features a salon dedicated to Guanabacoa's cultural exports – singer Rita Montaner, composer Ernesto Lecuona, and singer and pianist Bola de Nieve. The United Hebrew Congregation Cemetery, the first Jewish cemetery in Cuba with around 1600 graves dating from 1911, was restored in 2019. Museum entrance costs CUC$2, picture-taking fee is CUC$5. New York Times' correspondent Anthony DePalma's 2020 book *The Cubans Ordinary Lives in Extraordinary Times* is mainly set in Guanabacoa.

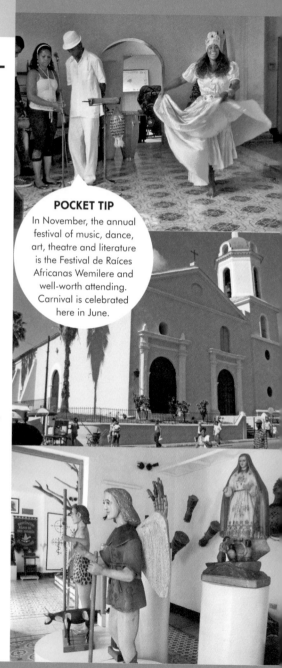

POCKET TIP

In November, the annual festival of music, dance, art, theatre and literature is the Festival de Raíces Africanas Wemilere and well-worth attending. Carnival is celebrated here in June.

4 REGLA

[MAP p. 190 B3]

Home to hip hop and a black virgin statue, Regla was founded on the site of a sugar mill in 1598. Today it's a town of fishermen and workers and its untouristy streets offer a glimpse of a normal working neighbourhood. As soon as you step off the ferry, you'll see the white Neoclassical **Church of the Virgin of Regla** dating from 1818; its interior boasts a Mudejár ceiling and houses a black virgin statue. The church is not only a site of pilgrimage for Catholics, but for Santería followers who come here to worship Yemayá (the matriarch of the saints of Santería, goddess of the sea, syncretised with the Catholic virgin), the Mother of Water for those who follow Palo Monte, and Okandé for the religious all-male brotherhood of Abakuá. A pilgrimage for Our Lady of Regla, patron saint of Havana's port, is held annually on 7 September when Santería followers clutch black dolls dressed in Yemayá's colour of blue. Carnival in Regla is held in June. Famous hip hop group Obsesión host an open mic session the third Sunday of each month. Check its Facebook page for information. To get to Regla, board the regular ferry (1 CUP) from the terminal (Muelle Luz) on Old Havana's port road.

POCKET TIP

New venture ReglaSOUL, run by a hip hop musician, filmmaker and holistic wellness champion offers alternative therapies and vegan cooking classes to Regla visitors.

5 MUSEO HEMINGWAY (FINCA LA VIGÍA)

San Francisco de Paula
7962 0176, ext 1
Mon–Sat 10am–5pm
[MAP p. 169 F4]

Visitors to Havana talk of the city as frozen in time and nowhere is this more true than at Ernest Hemingway's hilltop home. It's the details that make it so interesting – his weight and blood pressure marked on the bathroom wall, the swimming pool where Ava Gardner is said to have swum naked. The ivory 'Lookout Farm' is 12.5 kilometres (7.7 miles) out of the city and where the American novelist moved, with his third wife, Martha Gellhorn, in 1940, and where he wrote seven books. He left the property in 1960; it remains in the rigor mortis of 1962, when his fourth wife was required to donate the house to the government, with slain stuffed animal heads pinned to the wall, books and typewriter on his desk, and clothes still on hangers. A path leads down to the empty pool, pet graves and Hemingway's beloved fishing boat, the *Pilar*, in dry dock. Guides can be hired at the site. If it's raining, reschedule your visit: the shutters will be closed and you won't be able to peer into the house. Entrance is CUC$5.

POCKET TIP

The house is 30 minutes' drive from Havana and can be visited by taxi, or organised tour (arranged through hotel tourism desks).

6 LA DIVINA PASTORA

7793 7809
Mon–Sun 12pm–11pm
[MAP p. 176 C3]

This is the only place
I recommend to eat close to
the castle (Castillo de los Tres
Reyes del Morro, *see* p. 127)
and fortress (Fortaleza San
Carlos de La Cabaña, *see*
p. 126) – for both the location
and the food. Surrounded by
lush vegetation and a flank
of cannons, and reached by a
tarmacked slope leading down
to the bay next to El Morro, it
boasts winning views of the
Old City. You'll want lunch or
dinner on the small wood and
brick balcony that overlooks
the bay of Havana and
cityscape. Meals come with
complimentary bread served
on hot stones and a choice of
aubergine, pepper and herb
spreads. I've always found
their garlic shrimps very tasty;
I also recommend the pork
medallions on a bed of sweet
potato puree with caramelised
almonds. This state-run
restaurant also features
bar tables under parasols
overlooking the bay, and a large
air-conditioned dining hall but
it's the little balcony that's the
star location here.

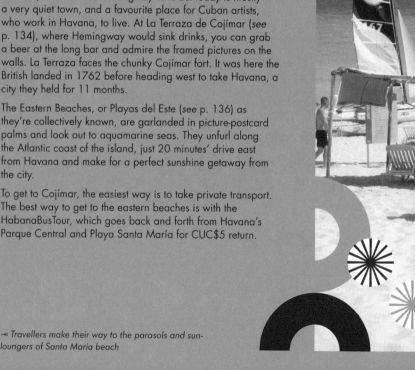

COJÍMAR & THE EASTERN BEACHES

Cojímar, an Atlantic coast fishing village, known for its Ernest Hemingway links, and the Eastern Beaches (Playas del Este), the most attractive curve of golden sand close to Havana, are both within easy reach of the capital. Ernest Hemingway kept his fishing boat the *Pilar* in Cojímar and the port was the inspiration for the village featured in his Pulitzer-prize winning novel *The Old Man and the Sea*. The boat's mate was said to be based on Gregorio Fuentes, who lived in Cojímar until his death in 2002. The port, 16 kilometres (10 miles) east of Havana, trades off its Hemingway links but today is mostly a very quiet town, and a favourite place for Cuban artists, who work in Havana, to live. At La Terraza de Cojímar (*see* p. 134), where Hemingway would sink drinks, you can grab a beer at the long bar and admire the framed pictures on the walls. La Terraza faces the chunky Cojímar fort. It was here the British landed in 1762 before heading west to take Havana, a city they held for 11 months.

The Eastern Beaches, or Playas del Este (*see* p. 136) as they're collectively known, are garlanded in picture-postcard palms and look out to aquamarine seas. They unfurl along the Atlantic coast of the island, just 20 minutes' drive east from Havana and make for a perfect sunshine getaway from the city.

To get to Cojímar, the easiest way is to take private transport. The best way to get to the eastern beaches is with the HabanaBusTour, which goes back and forth from Havana's Parque Central and Playa Santa María for CUC$5 return.

→ *Travellers make their way to the parasols and sun-loungers of Santa María beach*

COJÍMAR EATING & DRINKING

La Terraza de Cojímar (Calle Martí Real 161 esq Candelaria) is famed as the place that Ernest Hemingway would drink after fishing for marlin in the turquoise blue, or after ploughing the waves for German U-Boats during World War II with his Nazi-hunting team nicknamed the Crook Factory. A bust of Hemingway, created from the melted metal of propellers from local boats, is a tribute from local fisherman and is surrounded by eroded pillars. You can pay tribute to the author here, too, with a daiquirí at the long bar.

A breath of fresh air, diagonally opposite La Terraza, is found at new cafe and art space **The Way** (Calle Martí Real), opened by artists Alexander Rentería Castellanos and Alejandro Martínez Drago. They have filled this space with recycled and upcycled furniture and art. Sit down for coffee, beer, ice-cream, cocktails and conversation.

Casa Grande (Calle Real e/ Victoria y San Marcos) offers tasty moreish barbecue food cooked up by chef Jorgito Falcó Ochoa on its terrace with sea views. I vote for the charred octopus laced in aioli salsa, garlic, parsley and olive oil.

Popular **Café Ajiaco** (Calle 92 267 e/ 5ta y 3ra E) offers seafood and Cuban–Creole cuisine under a thatched ranchón (open-sided building).

For beers and German bratwurst on hot afternoons lounge about at **El Jardín de Bavaria**, Calle 5ta (also known as 28) 61 e/ Concha y Maceo).

EASTERN BEACHES (PLAYAS DEL ESTE)

The Eastern Beaches, with golden licks of sand shelving into turquoise sea and year-round calm water, are so close to Havana and easy to get to, there's no reason to stay. But if you fancy it, book into **Villa el Eden**, from where it's about a 20-minute walk down the hill to the **Santa María del Mar** beach, the loveliest strip here. (Note that there are no beachfront homestays at Santa María.) You can stay on or close to **Guanabo** beach but this is a very intense Cuban scene, especially in summer when the place is very crowded; the beach, with its burnt-biscuit hue, is nowhere near as beautiful as Santa María's sands either. Between Playa Santa María and Playa Boca Ciego is **Mi Cayito** beach, a favourite perch with LGBTIQ+ travellers.

I can't recommend any places to eat in Santa María so instead, I recommend taking a picnic from **El Café** (see p. 38) in Havana (but you can grab pizzas and piña coladas in scooped-out coconuts on the sand). If you do want seafood on the beach you won't get much change out of CUC$20. About 100 metres (328 feet) west of **Ranchón Don Pepe**, the restaurant where most beachgoers get off the bus, is a picturesque piña colada rustic ranchón (open-sided building)

with chairs in the shade. Watersport equipment hire is available on the sand, as are beach-loungers (CUC$2) and palapas (palm-leaf parasols). Move beyond the reggaeton blasts of the 'Tropicoco 1' patch of sand to **Playa Mégano**, which is quieter. Playa Mégano boasts more watersports options from its nautical point shack. If you come on a weekday you'll have much of the beach to yourself. Watch out for aguamala (blue barrell jellyfish) in winter.

Beyond Playas del Este is a large scoop of sand with a coral reef offshore, known as **Jibacoa**, some 60 kilometres (37 miles) east of Havana. There's a reasonable all-inclusive resort here, **Memories Jibacoa**. Five kilometres (three miles) beyond is the delightful fishing village of **Arcos de Canasí**, where you can swim out to sea, and dive off the coast into turquoise blue coves. Stay at **Montecorales** cottage for its in-the-middle-of-a-paddock vibe, and delicious home-cooked meals.

LAS TERRAZAS & SOROA

Buried in lush mountain forest filled with birds, orchids and dappled sunlight are the tiny village of Soroa and the larger eco-community of Las Terrazas, all just an hour's drive from Havana. The limestone ridge of the UNESCO-protected Sierra del Rosario protects small Soroa, known for its waterfall and orchid garden, and Las Terrazas, a larger hamlet of locals who live in homes and flats settled around a lake. Their idyllic rural life is the envy of many: it's the only place in Cuba where there's a waiting list to move into vacant homes but it's a tough one as rights go to family members and nobody wants to give up their bucolic spot. Fidel Castro launched his green revolution here in 1968. His mission was to reforest the area with precious wood (hardwoods the Spanish colonialists had stripped from the slopes), cure illiteracy and provide better employment for poor locals. Some 1,360 kilometres (845 miles) of terracing was planted with cedar, mahogany and fruit trees. All went well for this Cuban green lung until the Soviet Union collapsed and, along with it, the subsidies that had been pumped into the Cuban economy. This moment marked Las Terrazas' opening to tourism.

The easiest way to explore Las Terrazas is with your own wheels. The Víazul coach service also pulls in at Las Terrazas once a day. You'll need your own wheels to explore Soroa, or you can take a tour from Havana.

→ *The colourful homes of Las Terrazas' eco-community*

LAS TERRAZAS

Set around the San Juan Lake and with a backdrop of thick groves of royal palms and velvet green forests, I love to kick back in this relaxed mountain retreat. My favourite spot, after reclining in a bath in the community-run **Hotel Moka**, with floor-to-ceiling bathroom windows to observe nature, is to get a seat on the terrace of the country's pioneering vegetarian restaurant, **El Romero**, a short walk from the hotel. I tend to eat here whenever possible. It was established by Cuba's vegetarian pioneer, Tito Núñez Gudás, who began serving edible flowers to guests in the national botanic garden restaurant when Cuba's food supplies dwindled after the fall of the Soviet Union. I like to order the anti-hypertension drink and then tuck into organic vegetable dishes made using produce from the restaurant's organic garden.

By day, hire a guide to walk to the old **coffee plantation ruins** and prep your binoculars to spot the busy **birdlife**. The neon green golf-ball sized Cuban tody bird is incredibly cute. After a splash in Hotel Moka's pool, make your way to the **San Juan River** and do what the locals do, clamber in and lie back and chat, gossip and laugh in the natural teal-coloured river pools. There's a **riverside**

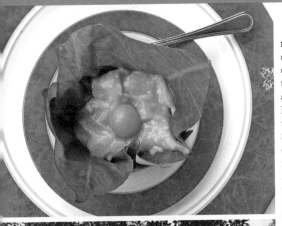

restaurant here and a row of cabins on high stilts for overnight stays, but I prefer the hotel, or a homestay around the lake, with their home cooking that beats the hotel's restaurant food. Seek out the locally made exquisitely perfumed mariposa flower perfume and the home studio of artist **Lester Campa**, whose canvases are filled with the fertile forest landscapes of his Las Terrazas home.

ꞘOROA

The 22 metre (72 feet) **Salto de Soroa** waterfall tumbles into pools at the edge of the village where you can take a refreshing dip. Nearby is the extensive orchid garden, **Jardín Botánico Orquideario**, with its 500 orchid species. When the weather's stinkingly hot in Havana, this place is a boon for cooling off. You might even spot the national bird, the tocororo, striped in the same colours as the Cuban flag. Book into the **Castle in the Clouds**, a 1940s mansion, now a boutique hotel on top of El Fuerte hill, with a restaurant and a small pool with panoramic views. My favourite place is the homestay, **Casa del Estudio de Arte** run by an artist and a teacher. Drinking and dining on their flower-stuffed terrace, as the sun goes down behind the ridgetop, is perfect after a day's exploring.

VIÑALES, TOBACCO REGION & WESTERN BEACHES

The early morning mist hovering over farmsteads at dawn, the pincushion mountains sewn with straggly plants, fresh tomatoes and basil for a leisurely lunch, the plod of a horse through the main street, the tinge of tobacco leaf in the cool air, and a mojito at sundown with the locals as you sway in a rocking chair on their porch. Welcome to the Viñales Valley. UNESCO thought it was wondrous back in 1999, making it a World Heritage Site, and despite the tourism boom since and radical upgrade of the main street from three lacklustre restaurants to a jumble of tapas bars and drinking holes, this place is eternally beautiful. Life follows the agricultural calendar much as it has done since antiquity. Farmers sew crops, gather fruits, tend animals and plough the ruddy earth with oxen, amid fields that roll around the base of huge limestone karsts – mogotes – hitched to the valley floor. Spend your days walking in the valley, horse riding, eating wonderful food and flâneuring around.

Cigar aficionados will want to nose a little deeper into tobacco land. The premium terroir that cultivates the tobacco leaves that are crafted into the world's best cigars is found south of Viñales at San Juan y Martínez. Viazul coaches leave Havana twice a day for Viñales; you'll need a hire car, or a taxi to reach San Juan y Martínez.

Don't miss Viñales' nearest sugar-dust beach at Cayo Jutías (*see* p. 147). You might hear about palm-strewn dreamy Cayo Levisa further north up the coast, but don't be tempted to stay the night as you're stuck with the abysmal food served up by the solitary government-run hotel. There's a quieter, secluded spot at Banes (*see* p. 146), closer to Havana, and en route back to the capital along the north coast, that's worth kicking back in – hammock provided, too.

→ *A flame tree graces the yard of a traditional wooden home in Viñales Valley*

143

VIÑALES & JURROUNDJ JIGHTJ

You can ramble out on trails close to Viñales town on your own but you need to hire guides for the longer 14 trails which wind their way through the national park. Call in at the **Centro de Visitantes** (Carretera a Viñales), very close to the **Hotel Jazmines**, perched up above the valley floor for information and booking (guides CUC$10).

Every casa particular (homestay) in Viñales can organise **horseriding** with official guides (CUC$5 per hour with horse and guide included). My favourite ride is a journey into the **Valley of Silence** to visit a cave where you can swim in the cool waters of the interior. Make sure you inspect the horses before you book.

Viñales boasts world-famous climbing for serious climbers. If you're a climber, the authority on this sport, which is world-famous in Viñales, is **Cuba Climbing**. For the rest of us, there's the 29 galleries of limestone tunneling at **Gran Taverna de Santo Tomás**, the largest explored network of caves in Cuba. For a glimpse of stalactites and stalagmites along the one kilometre (0.62 miles) that is open for visitors to wander, you'll need a guide (CUC$10; ask at the Visitors' Centre).

My go-to tobacco farm –
Quemado de Rubí – belongs
to Hector Luis Prieto,
onetime award-winner of
the prestigious Hombre de
Habano cigar award. You'll get
a fine insider tour of growing
Nicotiana tabacum, plus a
chance to see the work that
goes on inside a leaf-curing hut
and a chance to buy Behike 54
cigars that usually cost much
more when they're all boxed
up and hologram-sealed for
Cohiba. Dine on a Creole lunch
in the farm's ranchón (open-
sided building) for CUC$12.

VIÑALES, TOBACCO REGION & WESTERN BEACHES

VIÑALE/ EATING

The best food in Viñales is found at **Restaurant Cajuaní** (Carretera El Moncada Dos Hermanas), a tiny picturesque casa backdropped by a mogote (limestone karst). In town, head to **3J** (Calle Salvador Cisneros 75) for expert tapas and people-watching, while you sit on the balcony. For lovingly made Creole cuisine and an anti-stress drink at sunset, climb the hill to **Finca Wilfredo** aka **Finca Agroecológica El Paraíso** (Carretera al Cementerio). A cocktail or coffee at field-edge **Bar La Placencia** (beyond the end of the tarmac of Calle Adela Azcuy Norte) makes a welcome break after walking. Sip sundowners on the rooftop of **Tareco's Bar** (Calle Salvador Cisneros 75).

VIÑALE/ /LEEPING

Villa Secreta is perched on a hill above the valley, with outstanding views. It's an artfully decorated hideaway in which to sleep. **El Balcón del Ermitano** (Carretera de la Ermita) is a spacious secluded stay on a hill on a road leading out of town. In town, hospitable **Casa Deborah and Juan Carlos** (Calle C no.1 Final, behind the Banco Nacional) is the spot.

At **Banes**, about a half hour's drive west of Havana, and two hours north from Viñales,

there's a small laid-back fishing village which is popular with some of Cuba's biggest cultural stars. Kick back in the hammock and potter around on the sands at the **Estampa Cuba property**, a beach-chic casa (homestay).

CAYO JUTÍAS

You might wonder if you'll ever reach this postcard-perfect beach slipping into shallow turquoise sea, as the road from Viñales to the coast is pretty appalling in stretches, meaning the vehicle taking you there will likely travel slowly. If you haven't got your own wheels, the sanest thing to do is to book a return trip with the handful of agencies on the strip opposite on Calle Salvador Cisneros. It's around CUC$20 return leaving in the morning and returning around 4pm. There's no public transport option to this coastal corner.

When you're there, head onto the beach and turn left and find the guys barbecuing lobster. If you don't want to eat straightaway, book in, as these smoky beauties go really fast. If you're up for a walk, head all the way to the peninsula tip to see giant tangerine starfish resting in the shallows. If that's too much like hard work, **boat trips** can be arranged at the watersports hut on the beach.

147

THE BAY OF PIGS

Why would you holiday at the site of an historic world-famous attempted invasion? Well, if you're a history buff you might find a bullet in the sand, like I did, or you might want to visit the Playa Girón Museum (*see* p. 153). But, it's also because there's a neat little indie beach scene that's still a bit of a secret, some of the best snorkelling on the island and gorgeous beaches to discover by bike. And it's all just a three-hour trip, south-east of Havana. The Bay of Pigs is actually a large inlet punching up through the limestone on the southern Caribbean coast of the island. To its west is the vast Zapata Swamp (*see* p. 148), a national park in the shape of a heeled, pointed shoe, teeming with birds, crocodiles and flamingos. The area – with two large villages, Caletón (next to Playa Larga, *see* p. 150) and Playa Girón (*see* p. 153), in which to base yourself – is great for exploring, nature, history, seafood and for having an off-the-beaten-track adventure.

If you haven't hired your own wheels, the best way to explore the area is to get the Víazul bus from Havana to Playa Larga and Playa Girón and organise private transport on the ground. This is all very easy, once you book into a homestay, as Cuban social networks are extensive. Skip the two desultory state-run hotels on the beaches.

⇥ *Sun-loungers look out over the deep-blue Caribbean sea at Punta Perdíz*

THE BAY OF PIGS

PLAYA LARGA

The largest settlement in the Bay area here is the fishing village of Caletón, close to Playa Larga, spread out along a golden arc of sand. The snorkelling isn't good here but there are nearby spots for snorkelling (*see* p. 152). **Caletón** is the most fun beach to hang out, with beachside homestays, restaurants on the sand and live music under the stars. Nearby are the national park offices where you can hire excellent birding and walking guides. The **Zapata Swamp**, an internationally recognised Ramsar wetland, is home to no less than 18 of Cuba's endemic birds. The area is world-class for bone fishing and there's some crazy jumping tarpon to be found under the mangrove branches of the pristine **Río Hatiguanico** in the northern section of the park. If you're not an angler, the trip to book is to see the thousands of pink flamingos tiptoeing around the clear waters of **Las Salinas**. November through to March gives greater opportunities to see vast candy pink flocks.

EATING & SLEEPING

At Playa Larga, there's a strip of casas (homestays) right on the sand and on a parallel street behind. Stay at cute petite blue and white clapboard casa right on the sand, **Chalet La Casita**. Dine on the barbecue snapper at **Casa Sol y Caribe**, drinking their generous piña coladas at tables in their garden-patio overlooking the beach while you wait. Alternatively, book the excellent, spacious rooms at **Smart Beds Gran Hostal**, one street back from the beach, which offers good bike hire and top service.

SNORKELLING & DIVING

Between Playa Larga (see p. 150) and Playa Girón (see p. 153) are several snorkelling and diving spots. My favourite snorkel spots include **Punta Perdíz**, where you can swim over the wreck of an invasion craft. You pay entry for this spot but it includes lunch and drinks. The food is average but you can drink up the entry fee in beers or mojitos. At the **Cueva de los Pesces** cenote (which you can slip into with the fish), there's a reasonable onsite restaurant. Across the road, clamber down into the crystal turquoise sea from the limestone-sharp shore and swim with tropical fish. At both these spots you can hire snorkelling gear and book dives. There are some 30 dive sites and several **sinkholes** in the area. The sea here is famed for a huge coral wall; the drop-off is just 100 metres (328 feet) offshore. Ask at your homestay about the dive bus which picks up divers from the two villages and transports them to dive spots along the coastal road.

PLAYA GIRÓN

Known around the world as the site of the attempted US-backed invasion of the island by Cuban exiles on 15 April 1961, this place is remote. But that was the point for the exiles; they'd betted on a spot that was more wild bush than town, but Castro had got wind of the invasion and Cuba's new revolutionary government was on standby to repel the 1000-strong invading force. Some 160 Cubans and 120 of the invading force died. The Cuban fallen are commemorated by large grey stone monuments that you'll pass on the side of the road. The story is captured in the neat **Playa Girón Museum** fronted by a British Fury plane which sank approaching ships. Following the invasion, Fidel Castro publicly declared his commitment to socialism.

TRINIDAD & SURROUNDS

Described as the 'Florence of the Caribbean', this small city in Cuba is all cobblestones, squat churches and fancy palaces of pistachio, pink and ochre, and is a major tourist attraction and UNESCO World Heritage Site. Founded in 1514, Trinidad blossomed between the mid 1700s to the mid-19th century before the sugar market collapsed in the 1860s. Frozen in time – the mid-19th century to be precise – the historic core has survived major modern development and is loved by visitors. Come for the palaces, the European decorative flavour, flâneuring around the picturesque streets, horse-riding locals, the great live music venues, the beautiful Caribbean light and a quick jaunt to the beach and mountains.

Trinidad's gorgeous looks are the result of a 19th-century sugar boom powered by captive African slaves who worked dozens of plantations in the nearby Valley of the Sugar Mills (see p. 156). Many aristocratic homes – characterised by large wooden doors, outsized windows protected by wooden or iron grilles, tall-ceilinged salons, arches, medio punto skylights (stained glass half-moon windows), tiled floors, carved and decorated half-doors (mamparas) and patios – are now museums (see p. 156). There are many grand casas (homestays, see p. 160) and you can bed down in luxurious splendour at bargain prices. Once you've explored the small city and danced the night away to live bands (see p. 160), head down to the gold-sand beach on the Ancón peninsula, and up to the Escambray Mountains (see p. 158) to hike and frolic in waterfalls.

Trinidad can be reached with your own wheels, private taxi, or with the Víazul (www.viazul.com) coach service which runs once a day to and from Havana, and once a day from Viñales; there's also a connection to Playa Larga and Playa Girón (see p. 153); these don't always appear on written schedules but they do stop at these places.

→ A vintage American car parked outside a large Spanish colonial home

POCKET TIP

If you like festivals, visit Trinidad on Good Friday for the procession of floats, or the Catholic feast day of Santa Bárbara (4 December). There's a procession and bembé (drumming celebration) for Changó, Santa Bárbara's alter ego in the Afro–Cuban religion of Santería.

SIGHTS

In 1827, the Guáimaro plantation in the neighbouring **Valley of the Sugar Mills**, harvested the largest haul of white-pressed sugar in the world – more than two million pounds. Its owner Mariano Borrell y Padrón built himself a palace in the city, now the **Museo de Historia Municipal** (Simón Bolívar 423 e/ Peña y Gustavo Izquierdo; CUC$2), which heaves with decorative art, busts, and a reception room (read dazzling hall) painted in ethereal murals by Italian artist Daniel Dal'Aglio, who also painted the frescos (recently restored) at the Guáimaro sugar mill hacienda (estate house, see p. 157). Climb the tower for panoramic views of the city, coast and hills.

The other museum worth visiting is the 1741 **Palacio Brunet** (Fernando H. Echerri 52; CUC$5), with its Carrara marble floor, mahogany furniture, crafted porcelain and Mudéjar ceilings. Known as the **Museo Romántico**, the lavish furnishings were pooled from the families of rich Trinitarios. Palacio Brunet sits on the edge of the pretty **Plaza Mayor**, surrounded by the church, **La Parroquial Mayor Santísima Trinidad**, sky-blue **Museo de Arquitectura**, and the 1809 **Casa Ortíz**, now an art gallery. Climb up to the gallery's first floor balcony

to see the floral murals and city views.

The emblematic yellow bell-tower of the 18th-century **Convento de San Francisco** houses the **Museo de la Lucha Contra Bandidos** – the story of Cuban fighters who tried to overthrow Fidel Castro's new government from their base in the Escambray Mountains in the early 1960s. The bell tower views are beautiful. One of the best things to do in the city is take a **street photography class** with photographer Julio Muñoz (photo.trinidadphoto.com).

Base yourself in a homestay and head out on daytrips to the **Valley of the Sugar Mills.** If the vintage steam train is working, hop on at the train station, **Calle Antonio Guiteras** (phone 41996 368; or book through a tour operator) for the 30 minute-ride to the **Manaca Iznaga tower and plantation**. However, this plantation ruin with its beautiful restored hacienda (estate house), fantastic sugar cane crusher, and sombre slave-watching tower is oversold and overcrowded. You'll need private transport to get to off-the-beaten track plantations: the **Guáimaro** and **San Isidro de los Destiladeros** mills, especially. The latter is framed by the blazing orange petals of a flame tree. The government is currently restoring a few of

POCKET TIP

Trinidad's hustlers are professionals. Do not be sidetracked into ditching your pre-booked casa (homestay) for another by stories of homestay hosts moving house, dying or closing.

the haciendas to be small rural hotels. Book transport to the valley with **Trinidad Travels** (www.trinidadtravels.com), who also arrange **horseriding** into the valley, and **hiking** in the area. State tour operators have offices in downtown.

The golden sands facing a turquoise sea at **Playa Ancón** is not the best beach in Cuba but it's perfect for a lazy day at the seaside, and is only 13 kilometres (eight miles) from Trinidad. Get there on the **Trinidad Bus Tour** which goes back and forth all day for CUC$5 return. **La Boca**, with its shingle beach and locals' holiday homes, is very popular with Cubans; **Casilda**, the old port of Trinidad, four kilometres (2.5 miles) south of the city, hosts **La Marinera** (see p. 160), a great private restaurant.

The protected **Topes de Collantes National Park** in the forested **Escambray Mountains** shelters hiking routes, birdlife and waterfalls, as well as the surreal **Kurhotel**, a centre for health treatments, once a tuberculosis sanatorium. Book with state tour operators such as **Gaviota** and **Cubatur** (Antonio Maceo esq Rosario) in Trinidad for transport, hiking and waterfall trips to **Topes**, some 15 kilometres (nine miles) from the city. The most popular trip is the trek to the **Salto de El Caburní**, where the steep descent, scented

by the smell of the national flower – the white ginger lily – is rewarded with a waterfall and an idyllic fresh green pool to swim in. The hike through **Parque Guanayara** with a huge teal pool for swimming is also worth booking. At the far western edge of the park is **El Nicho**, a series of gorgeous cascading falls and teal pools for lazy swimming, buried in ferny, glossy foliage (CUC$10).

∫HOPPING, EATING & DRINKING

The exquisite work of wood sculptor **Lázaro Niebla** who carves portraits of the town's pensioners on discarded window shutters (Real 11) is a highlight for looking or buying. **Yudit Vidal Faife** (Simón Bolívar 294 e/ José Martí y Frank País) uses embroidery, for which the town is famous, in her artistic creations. **Souvenir markets** abound; buy beautiful light handcrafted lace cloth pieces from sellers about town.

Dozens of restaurants pack into Trinidad's colonial homes but the quality varies, so don't be deceived by funky appearances. The best is **San José** (Maceo 382 e/ Colón y Smith) serving up hearty dishes and seafood platters. Reservations are a must. Its sister restaurant **Adita Cafe** (Maceo 452B esq Rosario) is smart-casual in style,

159

efficient, with a varied Cuban and international menu, from snacks through to mains, and more centrally located.

Los Conspiradores (Cristo 38 esq La Escalinata) serves filling Cuban–Creole cuisine above an art gallery and the garlic shrimps at the 24-hour **Taberna La Botija** (Amargura 71-B e/ Boca y San José) are a winner. For affordable tapas and sunset views head to **Muñoz Tapas** (Maceo 476A esq Simon Bolívar). **Café Don Pepe** (Piro Guinart e/ FH Echerri y Amargura) is great for coffee and conversation in a quiet garden and **Bar-Café El Mago** (Ciro Redondo 264E e/ Rubén Martínez Villena y FH Echerri) has unique cool decor and friendly staff, coffee and music.

For seafood galore head to **La Marinera** (Jovellanos 178 e/ Iglesia y Perla) at Casilda.

NIGHTLIFE & SLEEPING

Trinidad bounds into life at night. Plenty of live salsa music, drinking and dancing goes on in front of the Casa de La Música on the steps next to the main church, known as **La Escalinata**. One of my favourites, though, is the enclosed roofless smaller **Casa de la Trova**, one minute walk away on Calle FH Echerri for its nightly live bands and dancing. Call in at **Palenque de los Congos**

Reales, diagonally opposite (FH Echerri esq Avenida Jesús Menéndez), to witness costumed folkloric music and dance performances.

Disco Ayala is a bizarre cave rave tunnelled into a Trinidad hillside: salsa and disco amid the stalactites, lights and sweaty dancers. Head north up Calle Simón Bolívar (Desengaño) from Plaza Mayor up to the Popa church. Follow the revellers for a further 100 metres (328 feet) up the hillside; keep your phone powered up to switch to torch.

Book ahead to get some of Trinidad's best accommodation. **La Casona**, a handsome hacienda (estate house), 10 minutes' walk from the historic centre, houses a pretty garden, stabling, horses, and rooms scattered around the ancient, artfully decorated property (Calle Frank País 759), www.lacasona759trinidad. com). **El Patio** is a colonial-era stunner with a patio garden (Ciro Redondo 274 e/ Juan Manuel Márquez y Fernando H Echerri, see: www.casacolonialelpatio.com) in the town centre. **Hostal Alameda** is an uber chic and charming retreat just off the centre (Calle Alameda 156 e/ Cristo y Media Luna, see its Facebook page).

GETTING TO & FROM HAVANA

Havana's **José Martí International Airport** (HAV) is around 40 minutes' drive from the city centre. The official yellow cab fare is CUC$25; there are no airport shuttle buses.

Terminal 3 is used by most international airlines but some use Terminal 2.

There are Cadecas (Bureaux de Change, see p. 163) outside Terminal 3 to exchange money, and a Cadeca desk at Terminal 2.

GETTING AROUND HAVANA

The first thing that you need to know is that public transport is complicated, and fares may have risen by the time you read this.

Taxis

Official yellow and black **Cubataxi cabs** are unmetered, air-conditioned and expensive (they will charge no less than CUC$10 to go from Old Havana to Vedado; bargain if you can).

Private taxis

Licensed **classic American car taxis** and primped-up **Russian vehicle taxis** (marked by a yellow and black sticker in the window – **Vía Libre**) are also expensive and will charge what they think they can get away with. Unofficial taxis of any make are unmarked and safe to take; negotiate as best you can.

Polished **American classic cars** (marked **Gran Car** on the side) start from around CUC$25–40 an hour and can be found parked outside hotels. New online booking site, GranCar.com, the Airbnb for classic cars, will launch in 2020.

Collective taxis

Almendrones (seen-better-days classic cars with taxi stickers/signs in the window or a taxi sign on the roof), also known as **máquinas** and **colectivos**, are less common than they used to be. They run on fixed routes across the city. Hail them at any point on their route by sticking your hand out and check where they are going (ask your homestay/hotel for guidance), i.e. Calle Neptuno, Centro Havana, to Miramar via Calle Línea and 3rd Avenue. Ask the driver when he pulls up next to you: 'Por Línea?' (Are you travelling down Calle Línea?), or 'Por Tercera?' (Are you heading along 3rd Avenue in Miramar?). The flat rate is 10CUP; 20CUP if you cross the tunnel between Vedado and Miramar on a long Old Havana–Miramar run.

However, recently prices have changed and the driver will often bark that your ride is 'un dollar' or 'un CUC'. (Using the word dollar to mean CUC is a hangover from the days when dollars were in greater use: they mean CUC$1), although dollars may be accepted. If you hand over a CUC and you're owed change, you'll receive it in CUP; drivers (choferes) occasionally pocket change if you don't know how to ask for change in Spanish. It's best to hand over the correct fare in CUP or CUC$0.50 for a 10CUP ride.

Taxi Ruteros (Fixed-route state-run taxis)

Yellow and black **Taxi Ruteros** (with more than 20 fixed routes) are easier to understand. They run 6.30am–9pm daily with a fare collector on board. Routes and prices are marked on the side of their vehicles with distances marked as fares of 5CUP, 10CUP and 15CUP, etc. The confusing part is they stop at bus stops, and other piqueras (stops), and other times they'll stop en route along the way if you hail them. If you don't see a bus stop, try hailing them. Note that after 9pm Taxi Ruteros can legally convert into private taxis (Vía Libre) and will charge whatever they think they can get away with.

Cocotaxis

Small hard shell yellow coconut-shaped **cocotaxis** are fun but not too safe, and the drivers always ask for exorbitant fares; best to avoid.

Buses

Many locals use overcrowded **guaguas** (buses). They stop at city-wide bus stops and cost 0.40CUP a ride. If you can get on, as they are usually crammed; pay when you get on board.

The red double-decker hop-on-hop-off tourist bus, the **HabanaBusTour**, circulates around the city from 9am–6pm daily. Tickets are CUC$10. It departs from Parque Central opposite the Gran Teatro.

Pedicabs

Licensed pedicabs – **bicitaxis** – are useful for long distances in Old and Central Havana. Despite their notice displaying a 'list of official prices', there are no official prices. Bargaining is expected. Fares start at around CUC$2.

Field Trips Travel

Take **Víazul** (www.viazul.com) coaches to reach many of the Field Trips locations in this book. Advance tickets can be booked in your home country. Rental cars can be hired through: www.cubatravelnetwork.com/car-rental-cuba.

MEDIA & TOURIST INFORMATION

The Cuban government controls the national press. There are online independent newspapers run by local writers and journalists. Events and reviews are found at: **Cubaness Journal** (cubanessjournal.com).

News and events in English on **OnCuba** (oncubanews.com/cartelera).

Certain music listings can be seen at **suenacubano** (suenacubano.com/cartelera).

Eating recommendations can be found on the **Conoce Cuba** app (conocecuba.com), which works offline; listings can be found on **Alamesa** (www.alamesacuba.com), too. Download free apps **Guru** (gurumaps.app) and **maps.me** (maps.me), which contain a wealth of up-to-date info on Havana locations.

CLIMATE

Cuba's climate is hot and comfortable from November to March/April. In December, January and February cold fronts bring cool evening temperatures. Rains begin in May, and prices drop for hotels and casas. July and August are insufferable, especially in the east. Hurricane season runs from 1 June to 30 November.

TIME ZONES

Cuba is five hours behind GMT and uses Daylight Saving Time.

MONEY & ATMS

Cuba uses two currencies: The **Cuban Convertible Peso (CUC)** used for 99% of your transactions, and the local peso, **CUP** (moneda nacional) which is worth 1/24 of the CUC and is used for things such as local transport and street snacks. They are both denoted by $. All prices quoted in this book are in CUC and use the $ symbol, unless you see CUP written.

US dollars are subject to a 10 per cent penalty on exchange in bureaux in Cuba; in addition to the Cuban bank commission you are left with CUC$0.87 to the dollar. In late 2019, the government allowed locals to buy goods in US dollars via bank cards. Price changes are see-sawing and dollars are being accepted in restaurants and other places at 1 to 1. The CUC is no longer accepted as payment past the gate when leaving the country's airports. The currency situation is changing as Cuba hopes to eventually eliminate the CUC; seek advice.

Bring US dollars to spend and Sterling or Euros to change.

Cuba is very much a cash economy. Bring as much cash as you feel comfortable carrying (US$5000 is the import limit), as debit card withdrawals are subject to heavy charges. Credit/debit cards are only accepted in hotels, shops and restaurants run by the government. Cards connected to any American bank can't be used. (Call your bank to find out about indirect links, if you are not sure.)

ATMs/cash machines exist around Havana but not in high numbers. Change cash in Bureaux de Change, known as Cadecas, or in banks. Some hotels have Cadecas but they are often only for hotel guests. The **Melia Cohiba's Cadeca** on Paseo, el Vedado, is open to all. (Bring your passport for all transactions.)

HUSTLERS

Hustlers, known as jineteros – literally meaning 'to ride a tourist' – are ubiquitous. They'll offer unofficial cigars, cheap restaurants, casas, transport, men and women for dalliances. They're persistent but harmless.

TIPPING

Musicians expect tips from CUC$1.

Tipping of 10 per cent in most restaurants is expected but not always demanded. Check your bill carefully to see if the 10 per cent is included.

Taxi drivers do not need tipping.

Tip $1 per day for chambermaids in hotels. Guides expect to be tipped.

The tip for using a public restroom is CUP$1 but foreigners are expected to tip between CUC$0.10–0.25. Do not fall for placing a CUC$1 in the basket just because CUC$1 is staring back at you from the bottom of the basket.

HEALTH, MEDICINES & WATER

Make sure you take out travel insurance.

If you fall seriously ill, head to the foreigner's hospital, **Clínica Cira García** (Calle 20 4101 esq Av 41, 7204 2811, www.cirag.cu/en).

Bring all medicines and hygiene products you'll need with you. It is difficult, or impossible, to find certain over-the-counter medicines.

Don't drink the tap water. Bottled water is expensive and occasionally scarce. Bring a water purifier like a Steripen.

Bring tissues for public bathrooms; toilet paper in public restrooms in hotels and museums is as rare as snow.

SECURITY & SAFETY ADVICE

Havana is a very safe city, even at night on very poorly lit streets.

Take normal precautions with belongings. Don't tempt opportunistic thieves by leaving cash around in casas (homestays) or hotel rooms.

Few vehicles offer seatbelts. Official Cubataxis (see p. 162) should feature functioning seatbelts.

Potholes are dangerous so watch your feet.

Havana is very safe for females and solo female travellers, even at night. It is safe to walk the city's streets at night, and safe to take taxis after dark. Be aware and act sensibly, though, as you would at home.

USEFUL PHRASES

Agromercado Farmers' market

Almendrón or **Máquina** Collective classic car taxi

Altos Upstairs apartment

Apagón Black-out/power cut

Arrendador Divisa B&B host with license to rent rooms to foreigners

Barrio Neighbourhood

Bicitaxi Bicycle carriage/pedicab

Bodega Ration food store

Botero Private car drivers licensed/not licensed to carry passengers

CADECA casa de cambio (currency exchange office)

Carro particular Privately owned car

Casa particular A private home with rooms for rent

Chavito Cuba Convertible Peso

Coche Car

Cola Line/queue

Comida criolla Cuban–Creole cuisine

Compañero/compañera Common form of address, as opposed to *señor* or *señora*

Consumo Price inclusive of food and drinks

Divisa US dollar/Cuban Convertible Peso

Efectivo Cash

Fruta bomba Papaya

Fula US dollar (slang)

Guagua Bus

Habanero/a Havana citizen

Jama Food

Moneda Nacional Cuban pesos (CUP)

Paladar Privately owned restaurant

Parada/Paradero Bus stop/Transport stop

Peso Convertible Cuban Convertible Peso

Por nada You're welcome

Que bolá? What's up? (What's the gossip?)

Restaurante del Estado Government-run restaurant

Socio/a Literally 'member,' used to address friends/neighbours

Temporada alta/baja high/low season

El último Literally 'the last': 'who is the last in line?'

Yuma Originally an American; now used as a term for all foreigners (extranjeros)

LGBTIQ+

Cuba is a very machismo society but important strides are being made for the LGBTIQ+ community championed by Raúl Castro's daughter, Mariela Castro who leads the government-run **Cenesex Foundation**, the Cuban National Center for Sex Education. However, activists at Cuba's first independent gay rights march were arrested in spring 2019; it was organised after the annual government-organised march (in operation for more than 10 years) was cancelled.

Havana's first dedicated LGBTIQ+ hotel will open in late 2020. Ydalgo's Penthouse in el Vedado (www.cubaguesthouse.com) is recommended.

PHONES

+53 is Cuba's international code.

Since December 2018, Cubans have been allowed 3G data (and now 4G) on their phones.

Temporary sim cards can be bought via www.DTOne.com. For US$25, a Cubacel Tur SIM lasts 30 days and comes with 1GB of data plus 20 minutes of calls and 20 texts. Pick up the SIM at Cubatur in Terminal 3 of Havana's José Martí International Airport, or at any ETECSA phone office in Cuba near you. To get started, configure your unlocked phone's mobile phone network to 'nauta'. Buy extra data via www.DTOne.com only (prices start at US$10 for 1GB); no additional calls or texts can be bought for this 30-day SIM aimed at visiting tourists. Check your balances via *222*887#. Permanent sim cards from the only state provider Etecsa for CUC$40 including CUC$10 credit for calls (take your passport) are available. Get help to configure your phone, and with the same Etecsa sim, you can buy data packages from your phone (for Etecsa data plan info, see: www.etecsa.cu/telefonia_movil/planes_y_bolsas). Top-ups for calls/data for permanent sims are by way of **Cubacel** cards bought at Etecsa/private street window kiosks, or online via ding.com.

WI-FI

Wi-fi is available in public parks and certain areas around the country. (Wi-fi spots are listed here: www.etecsa.cu/internet_conectividad/areas_wifi.)

If you queue at an **Etecsa** office you can buy wi-fi scratch cards for CUC$1/hr. In practice you're more likely to buy them from black-market sellers (due to the horrendous lines at phone offices) for CUC$2/hr who will spot you before you spot them at all wi-fi parks. Hotels have Etecsa wi-fi but via closed circuits meaning that you must buy a wi-fi card associated with that hotel (prices vary).

Many homestays now offer wi-fi via Etecsa scratch cards and usually sell them for CUC$2/hr. Install a VPN before you come.

SHOPPING TIPS

Cash is favoured everywhere, except in certain government-run hotels, shops and restaurants.

Rum is available in the airport duty-free but availability changes. Buy cigars, rum and coffee in the city. Official cigars will be sealed in a cedar box, stamped with a hologram, seal and now a barcode (see: www.habanos.com/en/verificacion-de-autenticidad). Check Cuban customs for export limits, and check your own country's rules for import limits.

Those interested in buying Cuban art should take a private tour of art spaces. Try English-speaking Sussette Martínez (sussem@gmail.com) or take a multi-day packaged tour with **Havana VIP** (artempocuba.org). There are restrictions on exporting antiques, valuable works of art, and rare books.

OPENING HOURS

Most government shops open 8.30am–5pm and close at noon or 1pm on Sundays. Banks and Cadecas (Bureaux de Change) are open in office hours; some banks (including the main one on Calle Obispo, Old Havana) are open later and a few are open until 3.30pm on Sundays. Cadecas usually close for lunch between 12–1pm or 12.30–1.30pm. Many museums are closed on Mondays. Smaller museums close for lunch sometime between 12pm and 2pm.

ACCOMMODATION

Havana offers modern and historic hotels, as well as private B&Bs, private apartments and next-generation private boutique stays.

The Cuban government owns all hotels. Some are managed by foreign companies in joint ventures, such as Melia, Accor, Kempinski and Iberostar.

Many budget places can be booked on Airbnb, booking.com or cubacasa.co.uk.

My recommendations for somewhere special, listed by precincts in this book are:

Hotels

Gran Hotel Manzana Kempinski La Habana, Prado & Malecón

Melia Cohiba, El Vedado: Plaza de la Revolucion & Paseo

Private apartments

El Paseo Penthouse, El Vedado: Paseo, Plaza de la Revolucion & Around

Casa Concordia I & Casa Concordia II, Centro Habana & Chinatown

Suite Havana, Southern Old Havana

Casa VivaHavana, Southern Old Havana

Twins, Northern Old Havana

Boutique stays & B&Bs

La Reserva Vedado, El Vedado: Paseo, Plaza de la Revolucion & Around

Gardens Havana, Southern Old Havana

Malecón 663, Centro Habana & Chinatown

La Maison, Southern Old Havana

Casa Vitrales, Northern Old Havana

Villa Portería, El Vedado: Plaza de la Revolucion & Paseo

Casa Calle 15, El Vedado: Plaza de la Revolucion & Paseo

Casa 1932, Centro Habana & Chinatown

Casa Bonita 23, El Vedado: La Rampa

Casa Lilly, Vedado, El Vedado: La Rampa

VOLTAGE & CONVERTERS

Electrical current is 110V and 220V. Plug sockets are predominantly two-pronged (Type A and Type B). Some hotels accept European/British plugs. Bring a multi-socket converter with USB sockets.

PUBLIC HOLIDAYS

1 January (Liberation Day)

Good Friday

1 May (May Day, or Labor Day)

26 July (Revolution Day)

10 October (anniversary of the beginning of the 1868 War of Independence)

25 December (Christmas Day).

The following dates sometimes bring Cuba to a de facto state of national holiday:

28 January (birth of José Martí)

24 February (anniversary of the beginning of the 1895 War of Independence)

8 March (International Women's Day)

19 April (anniversary of Bay of Pigs)

30 July (Day of the Martyrs of the Revolution)

8 October (anniversary of the death of Che Guevara)

28 October (anniversary of the death of Camilo Cienfuegos)

7 December (anniversary of the death of Antonio Maceo).

EMBASSIES

United States Embassy
Calle Calzada e/ Calles L y M, Vedado (7839 4100; cu.usembassy.gov).

Embassy of Canada
Calle 30 no. 518, cnr of Avenida 7, Miramar (7204 2516; www.canadainternational.gc.ca/cuba).

British Embassy
Calle 34 no.702 e/ Av 7, Miramar (7214 2200; www.gov.uk/world/organisations/british-embassy-havana).

There is no **Australian Embassy** in Cuba. The Canadian Embassy officially assists. See: smartraveller.gov.au/Countries/americas/caribbean/Pages/cuba.aspx.

The **New Zealand Embassy** in Mexico City officially assists NZ citizens. See: https://safetravel.govt.nz/cuba.

VISAS

All tourists need a 30-day **Tourist Card**.

British

For UK citizens these are sold by the **Virgin Holidays**' desk at London Gatwick next to check-in for £15 to Virgin Atlantic passengers. The cheapest online provider is: www.cubavisas.com for £24 pp, including standard delivery.

Other countries

Consulates or travel agencies in other countries sell tourist cards.

Americans & all travellers flying to Cuba from the US

Tourism for Americans in Cuba remains prohibited. Legal travel is available through 12 licensed categories. The easiest category for the general traveller to travel under is the 'Support for the Cuban people'. What this category means on the ground is that visitors need to eat at paladares (private restaurants), talk to business owners and craftspeople, interact with Cuban artists, for example, in a 'meaningful way' and maintain a 'full time schedule of activities that enhance contact with the Cuban people'. Keep detailed written records and receipts. You will be asked your category of travel when you book a flight routing from the US to Cuba. For detailed information consult the **US Department of Treasury** rules (www.treasury.gov/resource-center/sanctions/Programs/Documents/cuba_faqs_new.pdf) (§ 515.574 indicates Support for the Cuban people). American citizens, and those subject to US jurisdiction (see below), may not have direct financial transactions with any of the following: hotels, restaurants, shops and companies in Cuba, after President Trump tightened travel restrictions in November 2017: www.state.gov/cuba-sanctions/cuba-restricted-list.

Foreign travellers should note that if they fly direct from the US to Cuba, they are 'subject to US jurisdiction' – they are subject to the same rules as American citizens and must abide by the legal categories of travel – on paper. American airlines and agencies sell expensive pink-hued tourist cards along with flights. Note that the green-hued tourist cards, bought in the UK, say, are not accepted on the US–Cuba flights.

American cruise ships were banned from Cuba in June 2019.

FESTIVALS & EVENTS

There are festivals nearly every week of the year. Check **La Papelete** for the lowdown (www.lapapeleta.cult.cu). It's in Spanish only but organised in a way to be understandable.

Major festivals include:

The annual **January Jazz Festival** (festivaljazzplaza.com).

The **Wake of Pachencho** which sees the faux burial of a man, and street conga in Santiago de las Vegas, 20 kilometres (12 miles) south of Havana every 5 February.

Havana's March **Rhythm and Dance Festival** (www.fiestadeltamborpopular.com/en).

Ciudad en Movimiento sees a dance and performance throughout the streets of Old Havana every April, organised by Retazos theatre group (www.danzateatroretazos.cu/index.php/festivales).

The **Habana Bienal** (possibly now on a three-year rotation; the next one could be 2021 or 2022), where art and performance is staged across plazas, urban lots, the sea wall, galleries and museums across the city (bienaldelahabana.fcbc.cu).

The religious processions for the **Virgin of Regla** (7 Sept) and **Virgin of Charity of El Cobre**, Cuba's patron saint (8 Sept).

The **biennial international ballet festival** (www.balletcuba.cult.cu) is at the end of October.

The wildly popular annual **International Festival of New Latin American Cinema** (habanafilmfestival.com) is in December.

The extraordinary **Día de San Lázaro**, which sees pilgrims walk and crawl from central Havana to the El Rincón sanctuary, south of Havana on 17 December, to honour Babalu-Ayé, Saint Lazarus' alter-ego in the Santería religion.

Baseball: Check the online schedule (www.baseballdecuba.com/schedule) and with the locals before heading to watch the national sport. The season lasts from August through to March. Havana's Industriales often play at home in the city's Latin American Stadium.

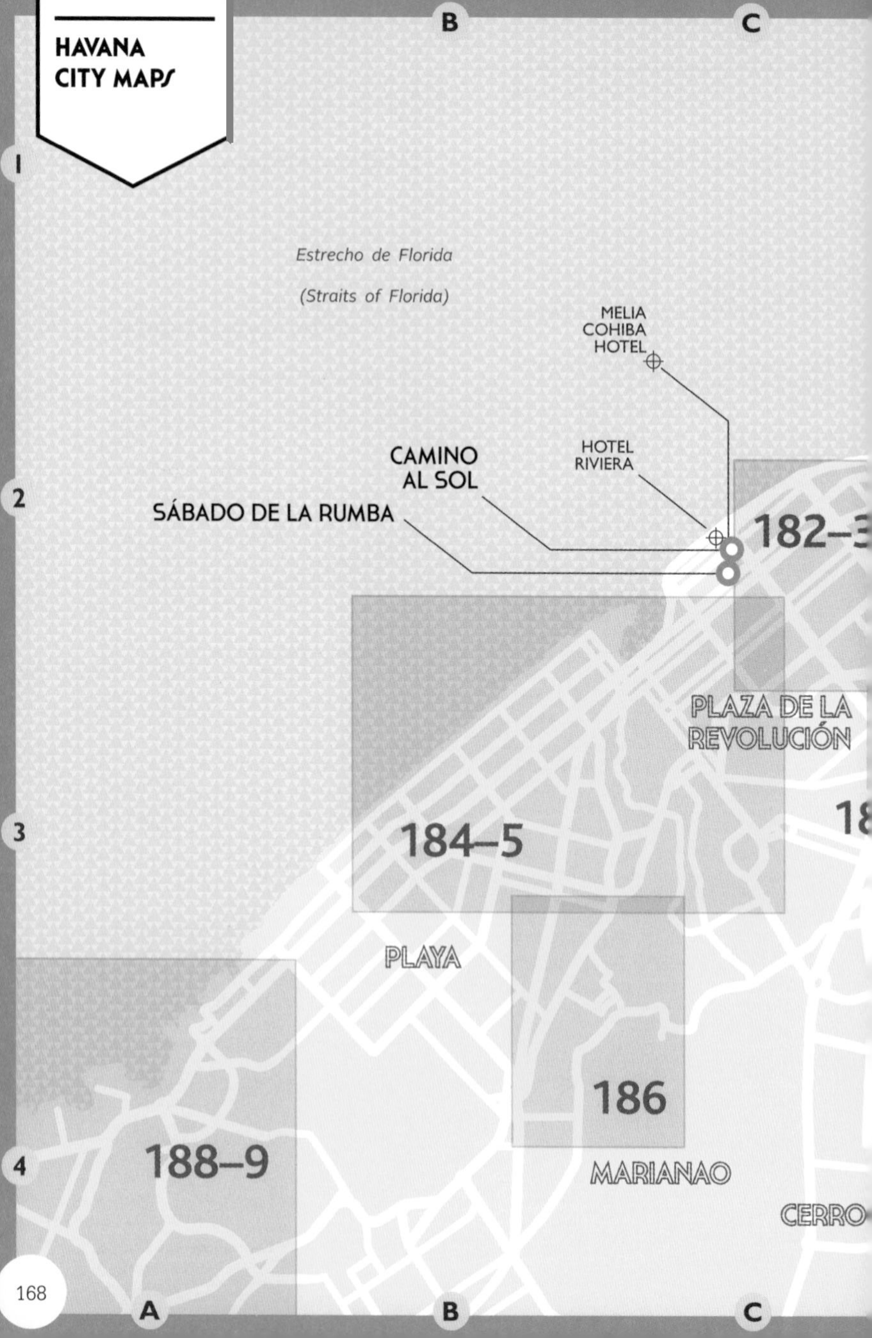

Estrecho de Florida

(Straits of Florida)

MELIA COHIBA HOTEL ⊕

HOTEL RIVIERA

CAMINO AL SOL

SÁBADO DE LA RUMBA

⊕ 182–3

PLAZA DE LA REVOLUCIÓN

18

184–5

PLAYA

186

188–9

MARIANAO

CERRO

A B C

HAVANA

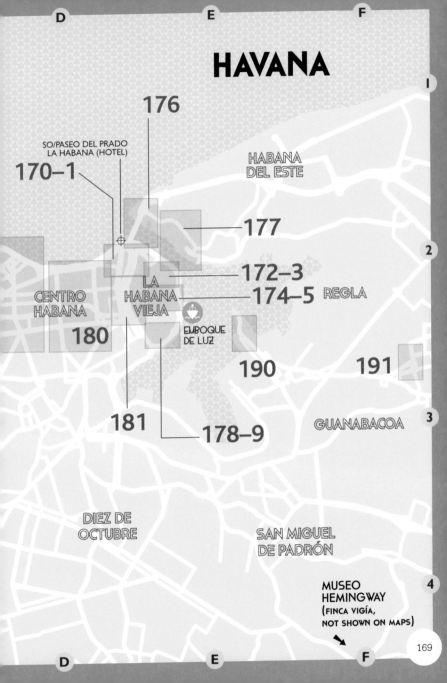

176

SO/PASEO DEL PRADO
LA HABANA (HOTEL)

170–1

HABANA
DEL ESTE

177

172–3

174–5

REGLA

CENTRO
HABANA

LA
HABANA
VIEJA

180

EMBOQUE
DE LUZ

190

191

181

178–9

GUANABACOA

DIEZ DE
OCTUBRE

SAN MIGUEL
DE PADRÓN

MUSEO
HEMINGWAY
(FINCA VIGÍA,
NOT SHOWN ON MAPS)

A   **B**   **C**

1

CHACÓN

CHACÓN

Estudio Ares
(Art studio
& gallery)

**Hotel
Palacio
O'Farrill**

CUBA

SAN IGNACIO

SAN TELMO

Parqu

Hotel del
Tejadillo

AGUIAR

**BUENA VISTA
CURRY CLUB
(BVCC)**

TEJADILLO

Centro de Arte
Contemporáneo
Wifredo Lam

CATEDRAL
DE SAN
CRISTÓBAL

**Palacio
del
Conde
Lombillo**

CASA DE LOS MARQUESES
DE AGUAS CLARAS (EL PATIO)

**PLAZA DE LA
CATEDRAL**

2

HELAD'ORO

BAR
ELEGGUA

EMPEDRADO

Fundación
Alejo
Carpentier
(museum)

PALACIO DEL MARQUÉS
DE ARCOS (ROYAL TREASURY)

DOÑA
EUTIMIA

CALLEJÓN
DEL
CHORRO

MUSEO
DE ARTE
COLONIAL

LA
HABANA
VIEJA

CUBA

PISCOLABIS

Parque Cervantes

O'REILLY

AGUIAR

JAMA

3

LAFAYETTE

CAFÉ
O'REILLY

SAN IGNACIO

O'REILLY

**FACTORÍA
HABANA**

304
O'REILLY

OBISPO

HABANA

Casa
Victor Hugo
(museum)

**EL DEL
FRENTE**

Hotel
Florida

CUBA

4

LA LLUVIA
DEL ORO

OBISPO

0   50 m

N

Museo
Numismático

A   **B**   **C**

OBRAPÍA

D

Museo
Simón
Bolívar

Museo
Armería
9 de Abril

Parque
Guayasamín

**CASA DEL
HABANO**
(OTEL CONDE DE
VILLANUEVA)

MERCADERES

**MUSEO NACIONAL
DE LA CERÁMICA
CONTEMPORÁNEA
CUBANA**

AMARGURA

E

**LONJA DEL
COMERCIO
(STOCK EXCHANGE)**

Hotel Palacio del
Marqués de San Felipe y
Santiago de Bejucal

F

**TERMINAL
SIERRA
MAESTRA
(CRUISE SHIP
TERMINAL)**

I

Museo de
Chocolate

**PLAZA DE
SAN FRANCISCO
DE ASÍS**

El Mesón
de la Flota
(hotel)

**EL CABALLERO
DE PARIS
(THE GENTLEMAN
OF PARIS)**

OFICIOS

BASÍLICA MENOR Y
CONVENTO DE
SAN FRANCISCO
DE ASÍS

AVENIDA DEL PUERTO (SAN PEDRO)

2

MERCADERES

Hotel
Los
Fraíles

(TENIENTE REY)

Royal Canal
(old aqueduct
ruins)

BRASIL

**CÁMARA
OSCURA**

Convento
de Santa Brígida

CHURRUCA

Plaza Vieja

⊕ **FOTOTECA DE CUBA**

Planetario
(Planetarium)

MURALLA

Parque
Alejandro
de
Humboldt

3

Museo
de Naipes

**Hotel
Palacio
Cueto**

**MUSEO
DE RON
HAVANA
CLUB**

A VITROLA

SOL

Catedral
Ortodoxa
Nuestra
Señora
de Kazán

IGNACIO

SOL

INQUISIDOR

OFICIOS

4

CLARA

SANTA

Madero
B&B

175

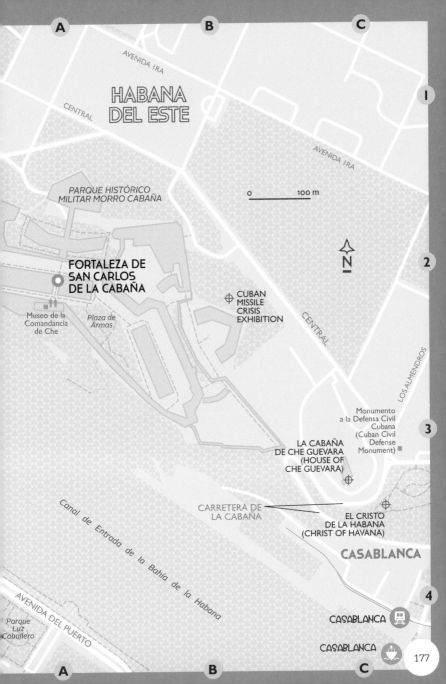

JESÚS MARÍA 20

JESÚS MARÍA

CUBA

MERCED

MERCED

SAN IGNACIO

JIBARO

IGLESIA DE LA MERCED

RAFAEL TREJO TRAINING GYM

Alameda de Paula

DAMAS

(PAULA)

Iglesia de San Francisco de Paula

LEONOR PÉREZ

CUBA

SAN ISIDRO

Parque de la Ceiba

N

DAMAS

ALMACENES SAN JOSÉ

HABANA

(DESAMPARADOS)

VELAZCO

PUERTO

0   50 m

DEL

Bahía de la Habana

AVENIDA

D   E   F

A
- ÁNIMAS
- MEMORIAS
- PALACIO DE LOS MATRIMONIOS
- SLOPPY JOE'S
- PALACIO BALAGUER
- LA TERRAZA
- VIRTUDES
- Leones del Prado
- Leones del Prado
- HOTEL PLAZA
- HOTEL ELÉGRAFO
- HOTEL IBEROSTAR PARQUE CENTRAL
- NEPTUNO
- PARQUE CENTRAL
- JOSÉ MARTÍ STATUE
- HOTEL INGLATERRA
- ESQUINA CALIENTE (HOT CORNER)
- CAFÉ BACO
- Museo de Bellas Artes (Arte Universal)
- GRAN TEATRO DE LA HABANA ALICIA ALONSO
- Cine Payret
- SAN JOSÉ
- Capitolio Nacional
- EL CAPITOLIO
- PASEO DE MARTÍ (PASEO DEL PRADO)
- AGRAMONTE
- BRASIL (TENIENTE)
- (ZULUETA)
- Teatro Martí
- DRAGONES
- Parque de la Fraternidad
- Hotel Saratoga
- Casa VivaHavana
- LA FUENTE DE LA INDIA
- AGRAMONTE
- (MONTE)
- (ZULUETA)
- MÁXIMO GÓMEZ
- AVENIDA SIMÓN BOLÍVAR (REINA)

B
- AVENIDA DE BÉLGICA
- EMPEDRADO
- EDIFICIO BACARDÍ
- SAN JUAN
- Gran Hotel Manzana Kempinski
- EVOCACIÓN TOBACCO LOUNGE
- EL FLORIDITA
- OBRAPÍA
- AVENIDA DE BÉLGICA
- LAMPARILLA
- Iglesia del Santo Cristo del Buen Viaje
- Parque Cristo
- EL DANDY
- LA HABANA VIEJA
- BERNAZA
- AVENIDA DE BÉLGICA (EGIDO)
- MURALLA
- MURALLA
- SOL
- LUZ

C
- VILLEGAS
- AGUACATE
- DE DIOS
- O'REILLY
- RAÚL CORRALES GALERÍA
- O'REILLY
- AGUACATE
- PATIO DE LOS ARTESANOS
- OBISPO
- OBRAPÍA
- EXPERIMENTAL GALLERY
- LA LIBERTIJA
- EL CAFÉ
- AMARGURA
- BRASIL (TENIENTE REY)
- CLANDESTINA
- (MONSERRATE)
- (TENIENTE REY)
- CRISTO
- VILLEGAS
- MURALLA
- CURAZAO

N

0   100 m

Estrecho de Florida
(Straits of Florida)

1

PLAYITA DE 16 ⊕

IRA

CALLE 14

CALLE 16

CALLE 18

2

CASA MUSEO
COMPAY
SEGUNDO ⊕

CALLE 20

MEMORIA
DE L
DENUNCI

0   200 m

N

CALLE

3RA AVENIDA

ALMA ◉

CALLE

CALLE 22

24

5TA AVENIDA

AVENIDA

CALLE

26

Parque

CALLE

CALLE

Iglesia de
Santa Rita de Casia
(church)

Miramar

Casa de
Argüelles

7MA

CALLE 22

Be Live
Havana City
Copacabana
(hotel)

IRA

✉

38

40

CALLE 36A

36

34

32

28

CALLE 26

9NA

3

AMIR
SHISHA ◉

✉

CALLE 30

AVENIDA

30

5TA AVENIDA

STA A

AVENIDA

21

34

25

MIRAMAR

42

PLAYA

36

AVENIDA

27

3RA AVENIDA

EMBAJADA RUSA
(RUSSIAN EMBASSY) ⊕

42

AVENIDA

✉

CALLE

42

4

5TA AVENIDA

5TA A

AVENIDA 7MA

CALLE

60

48

CALLE 44

13

46

15

17

AVENIDA 19

CALLE

46

44

LA
COCINA
DE LILLIAM ◉

PLAZA DE LA REVOLUCIÓN

CALLE 35

A

B

C

I

Sala Polivalente Ramón Fonst

19 DE MAYO

MANUEL DE CÉSPEDES

ARANGUREN

Teatro Nacional de Cuba

PASEO

AVENIDA CARLOS

CALLE 39

TERMINAL DE ÓMNIBUS NACIONALES & VÍAZUL

MINISTERIO DEL INTERIOR (MINISTRY OF THE INTERIOR) & CHE GUEVARA WALL ART ⊕

Museo Postal de Cuba ✉

INDEPENDENCIA

ARANGUREN

MINISTERIO DE COMUNICACIONES (MINISTRY OF COMMUNICATIONS) & CAMILO CIENFUEGOS WALL ART ⊕

Parque de las Comunicaciones

2

PLAZA DE LA REVOLUCIÓN ◎

Biblioteca Nacional José Martí

PLAZA DE LA REVOLUCIÓN

AVENIDA

20 DE MAYO

3

AVENIDA CARLOS MANUEL DE CÉSPEDES

MEMORIAL A JOSÉ MARTÍ ⊕

INDEPENDENCIA

N

TERRITORIAL

GENERAL SUÁREZ

Palacio de la Revolución (Consejo de Estado de Cuba)

AVENIDA CARLOS MANUEL DE CÉSPEDES

AVENIDA

TERRITORIAL

4

0   100 m

A

B

C

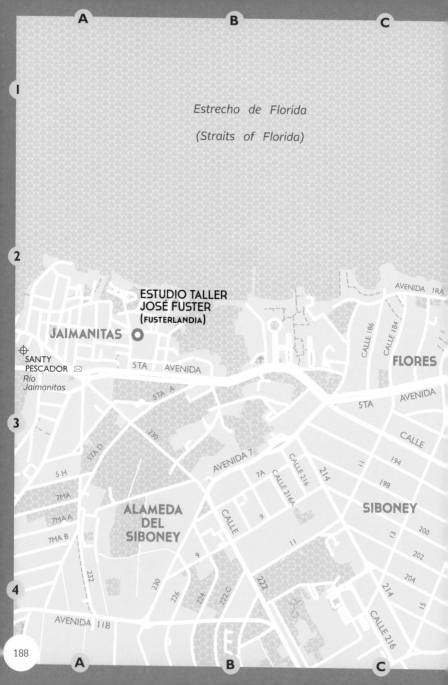

I

Estrecho de Florida

(Straits of Florida)

2

ESTUDIO TALLER
JOSÉ FUSTER
(FUSTERLANDIA)

AVENIDA IRA

JAIMANITAS ○

CALLE 186

CALLE 184

FLORES

SANTY
PESCADOR ✉
Río
Jaimanitas

5TA AVENIDA

5TA A

5TA AVENIDA

CALLE

3

230

STA D

AVENIDA 7

CALLE 216

214

194

11

198

5 H

7A

CALLE 216A

SIBONEY

7MA

CALLE

9

200

7MA A

ALAMEDA
DEL
SIBONEY

CALLE

13

202

7MA B

11

204

9

222

214

15

232

230

226

224

222 C

CALLE 216

4

AVENIDA 11B

TERMINAL REGLA

Bahía de la Habana

MARTÍ

IGLESIA DE NUESTRA SEÑORA DE REGLA (CHURCH OF THE VIRGIN OF REGLA)

SANTUARIO

LANCHITA DE REGLA

REGLA

GÓMEZ

MARTÍ

LA PIEDRA

FACCIOLO

Parque de las Madras

REGLA

Museo Municipal de Regla

GÓMEZ

N

FACCIOLO

MARTÍ

LA PIEDRA

MACEO

AMBRON

0   100 m

GUANABACOA

R. DE CARDENAS (CANDELARIA)

Cine Carral (closed)

Parque Marti

MUSEO MUNICIPAL DE GUANABACOA

GUANABACOA

Iglesia Nuestra Señora de la Asunción

Casa de Cultura Rita Montaner

Convento de San Francisco

0   100 m

N

Streets:
CALIXTO GARCIA, RAQUEL SUAREZ, PEPE, GARCIA, CALIXTO, (AMARGURA), FERNANDO FUERO, DESAMPARADOS, DIVISION, (CANDELARIA), R. DE CARDENAS, ANTONIO, CALLE NAZARENO, DESAMPARADOS, UGARTE, SANTA ANA, VALENZUELA (VERSALLES), MARTIN, MARTÍ, PEPE, ADOLFO DEL CASTILLO, QUINTIN BANDERAS (SAN ANTONIO), ANTONIO, ADOLFO DEL, CASTILLO, MÁXIMO GÓMEZ, VALENZUELA, GÓMEZ, MÁXIMO, MACEO, (VERSALLES), DIVISIÓN, PEPE ANTONIO, MACEO, PADILLA

ABOUT THE AUTHOR

British travel writer Claire Boobbyer has been exploring and writing about Havana for two decades. She first went to Cuba in 1998 to see why the Christmas Day public holiday had been banned by Fidel Castro. Within days she fell in love with the country and now divides her time between Havana and London. Claire has danced, dived, driven, drunk, biked and horse-ridden around Cuba, and is still discovering new corners of this enigmatic isle. She writes for a wide variety of international magazines, newspapers, online sites and guidebooks including Frommer's and Time Out, and manages the website insidecuba.co.

ACKNOWLEDGEMENTS

Claire Boobbyer would like to thank Megan Cuthbert, Alice Barker and Emily Maffei for their work on this guide.

In Cuba, she'd like to thank all the Cubans who helped her on her way, and specifically: Lilly, José Camilo, Thomas, Natacha, Lea, Sandra, Raulito, Julio, Amen, Diana, Luisa, Camilo, Jorge, Wilson, Hector, Sue, Richard and David.

Published in 2020 by Hardie Grant Travel, a division of Hardie Grant Publishing

Hardie Grant Travel (Melbourne)
Building 1, 658 Church Street
Richmond, Victoria 3121

Hardie Grant Travel (Sydney)
Level 7, 45 Jones Street
Ultimo, NSW 2007

www.hardiegrant.com/au/travel

A catalogue record for this book is available from the National Library of Australia

Havana Pocket Precincts
ISBN 9781741176636

10 9 8 7 6 5 4 3 2 1

Publisher
Melissa Kayser

Project editor
Megan Cuthbert

Editor
Alice Barker

Proofreader
Jessica Smith

Cartographer
Emily Maffei

Design
Michelle Mackintosh

Typesetting
Megan Ellis

Index
Max McMaster

Prepress
Megan Ellis and Splitting Image Colour Studio

Printed in Singapore by 1010 Printing International Limited

POCKET PRECINCTS SERIES

COLLECT THE SET!

Curated guidebooks offering the best cultural, eating and drinking spots to experience the city as the locals do. Each guidebook includes detailed maps at the back and a field trip section encouraging you to venture further afield.

These compact guides are perfect for slipping into your back pocket before you head out on your next adventure.

COMING SOON